A CHILD OF THE LIGHT

1-8-21

A CHILD OF THE LIGHT

A TRUE-LIFE ACCOUNT OF HIGHER WORLDS, ANGELS, AND SPIRITUAL AWARENESS

KATHY DARLENE HUNT

Ron, I am so glad you and cherie will be together soon

Kathy Darlene Hunt

ISBN:
978-1-954038-00-4 (Trade Paperback)
978-1-954038-01-1 (.mobi)

Published by:
Kathy Darlene Hunt
P.O. Box 44
El Cajon, CA, 92022

CONTENTS

Life is birthing us.

Our only injection that works miracles is a Light mixture released out of our precious nectar created out of love ingredients that only our internal heavens can make for us, as it is using our own life that delivers to us our sparkle-life where all life joins in being alive.

Our heaven's life is our creator. Our creator is the only one that knows how to keep us, its creation alive an' functional in all areas of our living ways about us. This includes our constant Light infusions that run our continuous Light-life that we are birthing out of.

Open an' read any paragraph—each does sparkle by itself.

A Letter from the Author

As I watch angels relay information back an' forth to each other, their bodies are glowing an' are transparent. So I can see their thinking arranging an' rearranging in many colors an' ways before the angel releases this message. An' if the circlets of information is not just the most purest in its living release, these angels' thinking returns back into the angel for more refining. When the angel does release this sharing, its beauty an' sensitivities is heart centered in a breadth sharing transfer that my eyes an' me are witnessing. These purities reaching into each other's angel life is overwhelmingly refined, pure love. Tears in Light is what I'm left with. So much beauty between people. This brings me a feeling of the visual of what our real lives are between each other. An' oh, is it nice.

As I'm looking at my visitors glowing in orbs of Light, I peer deeper into angels an' see a form of a body that looks like our form. But different in its ability to glisten in lots of jewels that are shining colors that form the outside of these friendly visitors into body shapes such as ours. As I continue looking clear through angels, I'm seeing a fleshly form. Then I am looking even deeper. This is revealing a skeleton frame at the core of these angelic visitors. Angels are made into an' out of life the same as we are. This is very peaceful for me knowing my origin an' family of Light that visits me an' cares for me in many ways. My joy in this way life is has me welling up with love tears again.

A

If all goes as planned, I am offering my book at various online ebook sellers for free, an' my print book at the tiniest price so these do fly to your friends easily. This then is a gift from my life to yours. So, I hope it works out just like I hope. An' maybe if I'm lucky my angel wings will go viral. Life has chances to be sweet.

Me an' little unicorn are so happy that our book of love sparkles in wings with freedoms that are twisting us into angelic ways of receiving colorful life strands feeding us as angels' arms are holding us in their love.

A sweet feeling in the air brings me an' little unicorn to a stop so Light words from our visits with the Light worlds can be joined in my crystalline thinking so these enlightened ones speaking from our last swirl adventure little unicorn an' I came from can be settled in my misty Light for future blossoming of me.

But not only this. I feel like a sweet presence is here to be my friend as I figure out an' understand better about what I'm hearing so I can write it down so others may see a clearer view of themselves as well. I am feeling a calm excitement in me. My miracle unicorn an' I are feeling softness from sweet love.

We are both sitting down in flowers, an' as I always love to do I am laying my head on my unicorn's tummy. I love to curl up with my sparkling friend, close my eyes, an' activate my knowing's on how life works.

I feel a love. It is a bit familiar to me, but more revealing than I am used to. I know it as the giver of life. An' I have all the knowings of how I became this way. My life always knows just what is to be. I am a pure knowing person, an' so are you. We are always alive. An' I am bringing my pond of my silver sparkling self out of me into misty form. As I get my first forming of myself into misty Light, I am thinking I have it made until I find out I will be enjoying more of myself that has different kinds of skills in me. So I continue swirling more of me into glowing, formed love.

Now I must continue. An' now am I to do this? My life knows just what to do. I have an inbred knowing on how to be everything to complete my inner self's inner an' outer skills of living. I am so happy to have all this knowing an' am getting right in action to revealing more of me to me.

An' what a jigsaw puzzle we are. These wonderful ways of us living is our natural inner nature enjoying its freedom in the Light ways.

I am releasing music out of me as I'm shining myself into little rays of sunshine. An' so as it goes, a misty forming of myself into droplets of glistening water an' specks of purity's rainbow air is me being provided for by my internal heavens.

As I go along, I am watching an' doing my own becoming. I am activating more of me. I'm blossoming my little self in fun ways, enjoying misty liquid Light in me, feeling my glowing, forming self within me an' around me. I keep blossoming myself into countless varieties of living things. I keep joining myself an' finding new ways of using me. This is so nice. My life is doing this all for me.

But now life's way is telling me to understand that it is time to go into the next Light level. So off I go in a new pool of Lighted ways. Joining with myself is the way of my life. What could possibly be more fun than this all is? What could be more fun than being rays of sunshine, droplets of water, an' speckles of air that is formed into misty angelic miracle Light? I don't know. But I'm going to find out.

There are these new colors beginning to take shape within me. Colors unlike all the rest. But I'm up for the joy this brings. There are little color systems forming out of these inner places within me. I'm forming myself out of glowing Light, an' my glowing orbs are joining an' are coming together making something new for me. I know I'm Heaven's Light.

I am happy being the sun shining on top of the ocean an' the rainbow colors in the sky. But now I'm becoming something new. I feel so joyous with the changes being something always angelically beautiful.

My new ways of living are now being the beginnings of all that goes into becoming, living, swimming, walking, an' flying. So refreshing, this inner soaring in all these new ways that I am being an' living. As I'm forming myself into them all in misty Light, I am thrilled at my futures in these new lands of becoming.

I am delicious flavors buoyantly generating yummy goodies within me as I'm living in new ways an' places, living with myself in miracle ways in misty form. I am enjoying every glow of me. I'm figuring this must be forever.

But low an' behold, life is pulling a fast one on me an' is saying, "You are doing such a fine job on yourself, Kathy. We are going to do something even with more Light ways involved. Remember, Kathy, life is creating for you a special way of living."

Oh boy. How is this happening? I love my life. I am having so much fun absorbing the sun into my

D

leaves, being playful with my angelic cubs, enjoying the scent of me as I'm blossoming into glowing flowers, purring my fun ways into special feelings, an' flittering my angelic wings into the golden sky. All of this is me. It's so wonderful.

I'd better realize that things are always getting more fun as I go along this journey of forming myself into misty Light. I am feeling this is going to be a whirl into my Light that I have never felt.

As always, I know life is always with me as I know I am life an' I can only stay with myself. I am blossoming out of vibrant life. I have every confidence I am going to be OK, so off I go into a new way of me being me.

The biggest joining I could ever feel could happen is happening now. Right now I am in the Light of myself weaving my life into the most skilled functions that my little love-heart can envision. I am busy making all inner Light hookups that will make up the entire me.

Oh my. What a task I am in now. I can see life is going further into the Light with me. Well, the whole me thing I am going through is for the only purpose of blossoming me into a living, completed, Lighted being out of living moments. An' the living moments that I am is the living moments I use to make my living, formed misty shapes out of. Wow. That is a mouthful.

I'd better get busy. I'm getting pretty good at this life thing. Just look into what I am being now. This is just one more Light move in me becoming whole. An' now I can see that this is not my last anything. So sweet, how life does the life thing. I can see life has many things for me to become in Light, but I must be attached in an allowing way to my Light self. I can see that now. This becoming is bringing me into the fulfillment of my inner Light's brain being completed in its readiness to sustain me as such a life as this.

An' so it is, I am spending many more moments in this skilled influence in deep pools of Light coddling me, loving me, gently moving my nectar within my precious sensitivities around this love of angels' ways.

So now, as I'm figuring, life steps in once more an' is saying, "Kathy, you already know this is coming. You are doing a fine job, Kathy, in becoming a fine life. I commend you on all you are becoming. Very nice. Life at its best. So, let's get busy an' form the finest you of all so you will live with life in your most functional self."

"What?" I said, even though I feel it is blossoming in me. "You know, Life, it's OK. You know why? I'm ready to entertain more Light."

"Yes, my little child. I knew you would be. It has been so long since you first were pools of silver that you can scarcely remember your beginnings in your birthing. I am now going to tell you how you can enjoy your beginnings. The birth you are birthed out of is pure you. The love you are is so nice that your real joy has taken flight into your forever function. You have you completed in misty form. The stable blossoming now begins your looping into forever's heavens. Yippee.

"You have a completed you to function with, that has all the ways of you becoming you. So you can now bring completion skills into you an' from you. You have all of you now to sparkle yourself into skilled, formed life. Because you have formed your own misty Light

F

that comes from out of the depths of yourself, you have become personalized. You are shining your misty formed self, your own living nectar, out of a misty form that you are taking into the next blossoming through an angel way of attaching into skilled completion.

"We do birth our completed misty form into a jeweled, skilled, formed Light body. Life an' we must do the forming of ourselves one sparkle at a time. What is a sparkle? A sparkle is our own skills that come out of forever living, blossoming, an' birthing ourselves out of our deep, thick, liquid-Lighted internal places. Our self is the stuff that keeps us blossoming.

"Our flowing ourselves out of liquid silver into misty form brings us into our beginnings of us being skilled form. So, as you can see, we will always be misty Light in our beginnings, drawing into us silver twinkle Light as we're sparkling our diamond clarity into forming our skilled Light brain an' skilled Light mind.

"Jewels of all kinds that we have formed ourselves into is why we shine like jewels. It's because we are the jewels that are shining. We are the butterflies that are flittering in the skies. We are something from angelic nature. We must keep going in the love of our own self. We are in the action of being liquid Light an' solidifying ourselves into being skilled Light in form.

"You are a functional life knowing all the things of how you exist. You are living it all. Sparkle by sparkle you are sparkling yourself together an' attaching your sparkling love into fun, joyous vistas.

"You are bringing your jeweled self into Lighted life lived in you an' formed into the outside of you. You are a joining in self. So you're living with Lighted, fresh new ideas about yourself an' fresh new ideas about your next Light world that you're becoming. You are bringing your entire life into you as your jeweled form is living entirely in skilled Light, Kathy. You're listening well to all of your sparkling instructions, Kathy. Life wishes you life's joys in the rest of your forever. A child of the Light you surely are."

My miracle sparkling little unicorn an' I are getting up from our slumber. We are feeling a refreshing aliveness. It is a joy visiting my birth. Off we go as we bid our flowers of such beauty farewell. The fairy people are all waving with beautiful smiles. As we enter our colorful swirls, I'm smelling roses an' thinking much Light is shining the skill for me to bring my miracle Light into words on paper.

I am having an inner questing about money. Money is our Light self's inner usage of its traveling nectar that is activating out of a natural flow in us. But when our money part unhinges out of its pure anything an' everything skill that it is, this money part of us stops providing for us in its miracle's natural function. An' our money part of our lifeforce that is our money provider part of ourselves changes out of its attaching Light flying ways an' becomes heavy.

So, our getting around ways like gold, silver, an' precious stones among everything else that we are formed into is no longer fluffy or a part of ourselves that we are utilizing in our miracle ways of living, but are now damaged in ways that no longer have the instant ability to stay intact an' useful to us in attaching miracles. Money is us, parts of us, rearranged an' coming out of us an' going through a rerouting long journey to return to us through many avenues that are no longer joined in miracle ways within ourselves. So we are not getting a direct line, or an instant manifestation, but are delayed through many channels.

All things now like our food, health, housing, travel has become slow an' heavy as we become more dense in form. My angel is popping in an' is saying "As you can see Kathy, these undoing ways are not easy. This goes for every part of ourselves. When we are joined in miracle ways, life is instant an' fluffy".

Angels receive food, housing, an' all travel from within themselves. Perfect timing. Instant travel through one's Light thinking. Instant feeding from within one's body. Light circlets become angels' clothing. Angels' housing springs from one's living in Light's natural ways. These miracle ways of being housed in forever living brings happiness to angels' way of being life.

I am releasing a joyous feeling. I do most graciously accept with love in my life as a means of survival of myself an' my angelic writings any an' all love donations into my life to ensure my way on Earth continues its pulse of love in a caring way. I do my best, as we all do in this visible life. I feel for all of us in this way of survival in sweet sharing.

Even a tiny penny has us sharing our golden nectar in visible ways with each other. Nectar is sweet abundance. Money is our nectar turned into our golden wings so we can fly in our earthly visible ways.

We are alive an' well. As we insist on it, it's our inheritance to be blossoming ourselves forever in fun's beautiful ways. This belongs to us. Forever take it, grab hold, an' always hang on. I hope to get my book in brail an' audio an' lots of languages. I hope someone will make movies out of these true happenings. It's so fun to hope. I am glad our lives are guiding us always.

Let's all keep breathing angel air. It's us attaching that keeps our receiving this beautiful air. This air looks like sparkles in pastel colors streaming into our bodies. This air is so clean an' brings us alive. Stay in awareness of it when it comes into you as you breathe, then you will be picking an' being choosy about the air you breathe. It's about "I like this sparkling air. It's easy to breathe. I like this inner sun-distilled water always being in me". Like, "I also like inner food. It's the best feeling ever". You an' I in a natural way are using Light, an' only existing because of our heavenly ways.

We are in control of ourselves from within us, being attached in what we know life to be an' what we know life does offer. Life is you, so go for the beauty of being aware an' knowing we are the ones bringing into action overriding skills freeing us, an' we are the life makers over ourselves in the Light. We are our own.

Heaven's message is strong an' clear. Because we're in a happy awareness, we're blossoming in Light's purities. We ourselves are the dictators, the priests, the rulers over our own inheritance of being miracles in Heaven's heart. As we are sweetly swirling in freedoms' healthy gifts for all 7,000,000,000 plus people, we're joining the ways of angels in their worlds an' star-sparkling ways into our forever Heaven's Light. Then it's easy an' fun to be living our life in our Light ways as we're joining angels' ways forever.

J

1

Sparkling in Light Thinking

This way of life is as much about you as it is about me. So, if we like, we can listen very carefully as we're sharing our diamond selves cloaked in angel shields that are encircling us in tunes of love as we begin. Life is made out of pinpoints of soft, sparkling love. What joyous aliveness I feel as angelic life is me speaking.

I would like you to meet my little unicorn. She's my twinkly ride. We would like to show you around our ways of Light thinking. Our ways of living are among angels' sparkles. Our ways of living are lived in the purity of our lives. Living in the depths of our personalized love is our normal way of living.

Hi Everyone. My name is Kathy Darlene Hunt. An' it's nice sharing these moments with you! I want to keep my words alive in the Light. The only way I can do this is to allow myself to join together with the abilities I have to bring forth what I am. I have put pen to paper with a message from my inner life.

I am keeping all the words the way I write them so that the messages will flow easily through to us. Since I have no education, my angels an' I are doing the best we can with what I have within me. These are enjoyable living insights that do shine lovely Light into the people we are. My joy is great being able to share my life with you. Thank you for being loving with me an' my writings, an' for touching my life. We are springing forth freedom in us an' around the world as we enjoy angelic Light angels.

My oldest sis wants us to look up into the stars an' marvel in life's beauties. I am 21. I go to visit my so fun oldest sister who is pulled over on a freeway in her motor home. My yellow 914 Porsche® an' I driving home, I fall asleep.

My car turns sideways. I wake up, semi-truck a few feet from impact. I pass out but not before silver shiny Light streams move me into shiny, glowing silver. I am being freed upward through the top of my head as my body is becoming living sparkles in miracle safety.

I am awakening with the semi-truck an' my Porsche® perfectly sitting at the side of the freeway. I drive home, sit by the pool, opening a letter from my childhood pal, enjoying the letter an' feeling as light as a feather. The air is crisp, clear, an' clean. It feels like love. So, so much love. We are lifted into miracle realms. Wow. Life has its way about it.

My inner Light comes to my rescue once again. Someone grabs me belly to belly at night. Holding me tight, so tight. An angelic stream comes out of me from my belly to theirs. I'm seeing my stream touching their stream with a hook at the end of it, dissolving the hold on several streamers holding me. This is melting their inner way of holding me an' dropped their arms as I run to my car that is running with the door open. The skills within us is the beauty of us being miracles.

2
A Touch of Me

"Everyone is like me," I say an' think to myself as physical people say to me, "You're so surprised people treat you the way they do. You really don't know!"

I wouldn't know. I am me, not them. I think, feel, an' know only what I am. I think everyone thinks an' feels just like me an' sees life as I do.

I always think all people are using angelic Light the same as me. I love nature, an' spend most of my time in it enjoying streams, flowers, birds, running, romping, an' going into places of love within me for companionship, peace, an' fun safety. I can always feel an' hear life within each person, animal, an' plant sharing in ways of naturally sharing from within us. This is my way of knowing life.

I seldom speak as I'm growing up. I let few words from people to have sway with me. It is a natural way of mine that allows me to live in a way I can relate to life better. My father tells me to listen to no one an' to do my own thing so as I'm growing up I can decide what it is I want to let into my life an' what books at these times I would like to read. Until then, Dad says, do nothing. So, nothing is what I do. I tune out everything other than what I want an' what comes natural to me like my white long soft-haired cat, Fluffy, playing in the rivers, listening to the birds, an' chatting with nature an' people my way. I can understand people better as it comes from the inner hearing.

The law does take us kids, puts us in foster homes because Daddy does not send us to school. Dad does break us out of these places, an' off we do go into a new state.

An' so it is. I tune everyone out an' live in my internal Light home. Life is fun in our inner Light places in ourselves. I live here, an' I can say that these beautiful Light people, places, an' ways are really here.

My father tells me there is this heavenly one, an' I will meet up with this one in my life. So, I can hardly wait. I'm 7. My dad never spoke of this again. Since then, I'm finding this one he spoke of is my yellow rose angel part of myself that lives in miracle ways.

I do not read words or spell. I am never taught. So as I'm sent to schools in foster homes, I do not let anything into me. As I'm sitting at a desk, I travel off into inner realms of Light inside of me till the bell rings.

My dad's father, through manufacture an' sale of the chocolate covered cherry, milk in a can, candy on a stick, among other things, amasses a great fortune. My father is Harvard schooled, an' swears he is not raising his kids the way he is raised with butlers, nannies, an' forced education. Daddy's mom turns all their wealth an' holdings over to an international peace mission movement after Dad's father dies.

I never live in all this wealth. I like living in these ways that I do. It is my joys in my life being free each day. Our daddy raises us kids his way, fishing for food, picking fruit, living on river banks in cardboard boxes. I am 5. It is so fun for me. Even as it rains, down the drippy box houses go. Sleepirg under trees, having soft, puffy clouds with so many fun shapes to carry me into sleep. Beauteous mountains with dear, owls, an' hot springs to play in. My daddy feeling free living off the land an' playing his ukulele.

I have an amazing life an' I love it very much. As I'm sitting on a rock in the river, having my feet in the soothing waters, listening to this water rolling by, I'm 15 by now an' my daddy is in a place called "dead." I know he is not dead because I see him in my mind an' dreams very much alive an' active.

I want the people where he is at to let him go so he can come home. It is different for me because I've never seen his physical body any way but alive, an' so seeing him active in Light worlds in my mind an' chatting with him makes it like this for me.

I am 11 an' in a foster home when my daddy dies, so I am only in my own private ways of knowing life. After Daddy dies, I'm sent home to live with Mom.

One beautiful day an idea trickles into my head while I'm sitting in the middle of the river on a rock to read the book *True Grit,* an' then go see the movie at the theater with John Wayne on the screen, an' see what the difference is between a book an' a movie.

I jump up off this rock, run home, ask Mom if she would get me the book an' take me to see the movie after I read this book.

She is smiling. She has been trying to get me to read for years. But as I'm not ready an' no one can take away from me my gift from my dad, my ticket to a free life to do an' think in my own head as I see fit. Oh yes, people try. Some are lawyers, judges, foster-care people, principals, teachers, friends, police, an' preachers. My head is my home. Being this free as a child an' a young girl is like the best life ever.

I begin looking at the black ink in this little book right away. Cover to cover. I'm absorbing every living image through my eyes. I can feel everything the characters are going through as if they are real people. I'm seeing in living color, feeling lots of stuff as if it is happening right this moment. This is so much fun for me.

It's all coming alive with such detail that it is something I have never been through in quite the same way before, other than one day Daddy caught my middle sis reading me a little children's story as we were hiding in the car so Daddy would not know about this little hidden book Sis has. She loves reading, even as a teeny girl. She is following our mom around, trying to get my mommy to read with her. Daddy caught us, an' this is the last story Sis ever has to read to me. It is gone now. What a sad thing. I do not think that I could not read, so when I have an idea to read *True Grit* I just look into the book an' it quickly enters an attachment an' with ease I become a part of the story. So many things changed in the movie so it is a bit of a dance for me as I am watching the differences in the book an' movie. Such a wondrous journey though.

My life is filled with many wonderful surprises. An' I do not think about them. They just happen. I think it, I do it, an' all is well. My life is like this. Isn't yours? I think it is. It's just that because I am given the OK from within myself to be the way I am, angels always bring me people that will care for me so I can live my journey of my forever life my way. Life has a way about it that is very accommodating. Life is sparkling out of a flowing action that is carrying me along. I feel now that I know better than to think that we all are at the same place in our forever living. I can be more a person of skilled love when it comes to sharing.

There has always been love from me, but now I have words to bring about chatting in ways of being able to talk to levels of people's lives from an internal point of view. It's nice for me to not just be love an' see love in people, but to know people have their own ways of living that they are living in an' special ways they are raised. These ways are our fun with each other as we feel each other's Light bursting out into laughter an' feelings as we're becoming different in each other's company as our Light mixes in miracle ways.

On the front cover is a picture of me as I am a little girl. My mother is a professional photographer an' she takes it for me a lot of decades ago. I'm still the same delicate twinkle I am as a child, as this is the case for all of us. The back-cover picture is taken 2019.

This is so fun for me. An arm swung at my middle sister. I see it, an' stop it. I am 150 miles from her. Wow. It's good living in miracle ways.

I would like to say here that a part of one's self that is in harmony with another part of one's self brings a sharing that is used in the depths of our lives. Hooking up with all levels of our self brings fulfilment an' completion to our abilities to function in so many wondrous ways.

3
Yellow Rose Angel

I'm living life with angelic attaching as I flitter deeper into my glorious ways of thinking in a Light place with so much fun. It's where my friends are living in their pristine enjoyment of natural functions. I'm going far, far within me. It takes love, a lot of love, to get me here. I am so happy. My joy easily bubbles out of me. I go about my days playing with the butterflies an' lady bugs, laughing, dancing, twirling, an' feeling good.

I find a girl crying. She begins telling me, "Since my daddy died, I can't seem to get my life together."

I feel love for this girl, so I ask my miracle land of love just what to do. An' my yellow rose angel appears. She is all aglow with sparkling love.

I ever so enjoy this wonderful part of me. She always has an aroma like a yellow rose. She is so kind an' ever so giving in fun ways.

My sweet rose angel is saying to me, "Dear Kathy, when your new little friend's daddy is going through the dying change, he is scared. He knows not what to do. He is alive, but knows not where he is. He is sad an' crying, so he turns to his lovely daughter of 15 that he knows loves him so much an' decides to stay with her awhile till he can figure out what to do."

"Oh, but sweet angelic sparkle friend, it seems to me that she would be so happy because she has her daddy right there with her, an' she says she loves him so much."

"Sweet little Kathy," as my angel puts her beautiful angelic love around me. "Let's sit down here by the creek on this soft, pink grass an' smell in the lilacs while I explain what it is I would like you to do."

Oh, I'm so excited. I am going to get to do something. I love doing things. I love it so much. I like playing in life's beautiful colors an', well, what I really like is using this most fun miracle love that is all around me an' within me. I had better put some good allowing attaching to what I am about to hear because I know this sparkling love can make anyone live more sweetly if it's used in just the right way.

An' oh, I would sure like to use this sparkle love in me in just the right ways. As my yellow rose angel is telling me just what she would like me to do, we join where the girl is an' find her still sobbing.

You see, this time my angelic angel is with me. An' before I know it, two more very large an' multicolored angels are with us. They have their rainbow colors outstretched an' encircling us with their love as they are sharing colorful Light streamers into the girl.

I am using myself as a soft, sparkling beam. As I touch the girl's inner Light to see the issue, color sparkles begin bringing in the color streams from the angelic ones in a sharing of my life an' my Light self to join into the girl's misty an' skilled Light self where I am able to see her daddy attached to her unskilled Light self. I am using my skilled Light as a freeing color to stream a crystalline bridge for her daddy to be guided into the Light of himself. It is tedious attaching coming out of our jeweled minds, fun for me an' benefit for all.

As this is going on, the girl says, "I am very sleepy." The Light rays an' my freeing Light entering this girl, it's taking just a few minutes. As this is being done, the angels are lifting this daddy out of this girl's life an' is taking him into their Light with them as he stays attached an' participates. So, off they go.

Now that this girl's daddy is no longer with her, she can use some freshening up. An' the angelic Light is letting me encircle life's colors in bringing fine threads of Light to areas of this girl's self that is using our colors. It is great fun. I enjoy using life's colors so much. The girl is telling me she is 25 now an' has her life back. But she is saying it's as though she lost 10 years of her time on earth.

So as my yellow rose angel is saying, "It's so much better if we would understand ourselves as living always, an' to enjoy our foreverness about the afterlife before we die so that we can know better than to attach ourselves to our friends or family members because as you are seeing, Kathy, it puts much unhappy on them an' changes the course of their lives".

We all have these skills an' many other skills. So, let's get to know ourselves.

Some things I love so much, like grabbing a bottle of distilled water, a pan, an' rubbing my hair an' skin in the water. Bath. Ears. Teeth. Drink. Why? Because it is clean an' feels perfect to me. I wear flat shoes with thin natural souls because my body loves it this way as it lets Earth's aliveness into my feet.

It's best for me sleeping alone so I can move around as much as I like. Sleeping curled up on my sides brings my Light into extra flowing action while I am asleep. I do it because it activates the heavenly miracle flow in me. I like a breeze bringing me its life's sweetness in the air as I sleep.

I really enjoy leaving my hands resting over my face after jumping into bed, or putting my hands on my ears. This feels like a protective, soothing love as I go into sleep. I think about the sun as my hands rest gently over any part of me in a comfy way. This feeling from my hands carries me into sleep. So nice.

Birds an' butterflies, I chase them. It's so fun. An' they love me doing it. Love is so fun to use. We can blossom lots of it all day long if we like. Love is something that just keeps on making us feel droplets from Heaven's sweetness.

It's really fun eating a little something every other day. As kids, food was not always around.

Eating one kind of a thing at a meal brings peace. As kids, it worked real well because having one thing to eat was a normal happening.

I'm feeling so hungry. A young, beautiful man with white shiny hair an' pure blue eyes kindly reaching out an' is handing me a banana, an' vanishes just as he came from miracle realms.

A way to enjoy these sparkle words in this book is in a way of absorbing an' attaching through this looking glass in these words as we open the ways we live through our own angel sparkle doorway.

4

Streamers of Gold

Life does stuff through us, around us, an' in us.

I'm happening upon a girl talking about a little baby that is going to be going into surgery. I'm thinking, "Oh, my. What a sad thing." I go to my miracle place within me an' ask if there isn't something that could be done for this baby so she wouldn't have to go through such a thing. As I ask, my Light thinking goes into my land of love.

A skilled, golden Light streamer quickly releases out from within me into the air an' travels to the people that are talking about this little baby girl. These golden, moving circlets begin swirling around several inches above one of their heads, an' this golden streamer then travels into the baby they are talking about. My land of love is releasing golden streamers as it has the action of change.

I do see this golden Light forming into patterns inside the baby. This Light uses its skills to work with this lifeforce in the baby taking, in our time, a teeny bit of a second. It is done at such speeds that it is eye sparkling to watch an' be a part of such a glorious happening. These angelic ones let me know that new findings will show this child is fine now. The joy an' the love that each one of us has inside of us is plenty to share with each other, an' it's so fun to do so.

We enjoy our immaculate clarity as our skills activate, then Light springs in our internal access of ourselves. The same is for our own self asking our self to spring Light in our self. All Light comes as a natural way to continue our forever us. We come from ways of miracles filling us with loving beginnings. As life is all in Light, we will not use each other. We will do life the Light way, an' all will always be Light for us.

People that have Light skills release their Light for people all the time, an' a lot of the people they touch never know. That's the internal way about life.

We are miracle people. Much about what we do we don't even know because our bodies an' minds are clogged with things we put into them. To remove these clogs, one can give themselves more moments of putting nothing in the body an' nothing in the mind.

So if we cater to our Light, we will have a self that can receive our own signals an' the signals of the parts of people that are made of skilled Light. Then we can share together in the ways of Light that are within us in an easy, automatic, natural way from the miracles that spring up from within us. Our inner nectar feeds us an' makes our water. This is the way angels are fed.

We also are fed these same ways. Our food is our colors. As our colors flow, we are moistened an' nourished. So as I wear cotton clothing with colors an' patterns of my proper Light self, I'm filling in between me skilled an' me unskilled by bringing me more ways for my Light to join my unskilled ways. On my back in bed, I move like I'm running. It's a gentle way to run.

5
Lasting Love

There is this man with tears dripping down his face. He is saying to me, "My father died."

Oh my. Right away I'm entering into myself. A life color opens, an' the love of this man's father is so strong for his son that I'm feeling it in a deep way. I'm seeing an' hearing his father trying to speak to his son, but his son cannot hear his father.

So my Light is instructing me to share in their life which I'm so happy to do. This man's father is letting me hear his thinking an' feel his feelings. I begin relaying the same thinking an' feelings to his son through words. The love in the room feels so wonderful.

"Do you remember when you were a little boy an' growing up what the first thing I did was when I came through the door when I got home from work?"

This man is looking at me with a surprising look an' is saying, "My dad always greets me by coming over to me first before anyone else to hug me an' see how things are going with me."

"Well, this is your dad's way of giving you love. An' your father is here right beside you an' wants you to know his special way of his love. Your father is so happy to be enjoying these precious moments with you right now." The love is so strong that this son's face is streaming with tears, an' his father is smiling with pure joy to complete his earthly desire which is letting his son know the way he shows h s love to him.

An' he will continue to show his love, even in his new invisible form he finds himself in. There is a bond of love that continues on. "I love you son."

This has shown me to see that each of us has our own unique way of giving love. I like being a part of people's fun love, an' I so enjoy my connections with real Light angelic people. It is a nice sharing in my life.

When it's loving an' springs up out of love, there is safety in sharing with people. Love is a protective force, a kind force, a reliable force, a force that brings our always being there in each other's reach so we can continue our relationships in a fun, an' always in the now, bond.

I always feel coddled an' at peace in my inner mind within my miracle garden of love. Sweet Light worlds an' friends are always here for us to enjoy.

A wow thing. I was sleeping an' saw my brother being killed on a motorcycle. I woke up in a sweat. I was 15 at the time, an' knew it was real. I asked my Light through my feelings an' tears if it would not let this happen. Years later my brother said to me he had planned to take a trip on a motorcycle but never did.

This is some fun in my bed. I feel myself part in my sleep an' part awake. I'm traveling through a distance, an' leaving a brown bag with a pair of swim trunks in it. The next day, a friend arrives with bag, an' trunks to swim. My life did that. Wow.

6

Sleeping an' Light Fun

As I'm sleeping, I find myself in a crystalline classroom filled with shine, with me sitting in a school desk made out of diamond angels. I'm deeply quivering in love tears as these angels' soul-life rays are changing my life that I'm reforming. This golden silver rainbow diamond angelic Light fills me as my sun rearranges me in my inner blossoming. As I am awakening, I'm feeling tears on my face an' am feeling ever so wonderful.

This classroom is lit in orbs of soft love. Each of our diamond desks have living abilities that life arranges for us to sit in so we are receiving deeply from our inner Light's self-made inner current.

Life just appears to us, an' then vanishes in twinkles as life's sparkles stop releasing its life's ways to me an' the others. Life shares into our Light as it is very delicate with us. Life's beauty is very giving.

There is automatic Life to make everything happen. Some parts of us are living in these levels, an' are aware of travel from earthly lives in sleep to participate in ways of sharing with ourselves.

Life assists children to be able to come an' go, an' brings sparkling fun areas alive with colors releasing into these children as important sharing.

Life is evolving its ways as it is bringing exciting intervening miracles into the lives of everyone that comes into it while they're asleep or awake.

These places are blossoming in the same moments that oneself is blossoming. These lovely places are always open to new sparkles. Each one has a special sparkle that comes from their joyous life that they do share.

Life is always rolling its Light around us as we are pitching in an' becoming a regular here in these wonderful places from within us. We all have very special places that belong to us. Living within is fun. I am breathing in the sweet aromas of the flowers, an' enjoying the thinking Light water falling over the shiny hills.

As I'm awakening on Earth, I'm deciding to grab a pen an' paper, an' sparkle within my mind to have some Light fun. So up I go onto my diamond saddle that little unicorn is wearing, an' we prance off enjoying the fun of the miracle day.

I begin seeing little fountains of Light that is dancing an' singing with itself. This watery liquid is alive an' actually having fun. I'm getting off of little unicorn an' going over to play with this shiny water. My bare feet are enjoying touching this soft, sparkling ground. The sparkles are tingly on my feet as I keep running to put myself into the pond of clear, blue water. The water is splashing an' giggling. What a joyous surprise. The water is actually playing with me an' knows I'm here. I am giggling so much while I am being splashed an' falling down in the pond, feeling so loved. I see angelic people coming an' going as each angel is so very different in their Lighted, formed appearance.

My little unicorn took off for a few moments but came back. She is beautiful. She is a miracle of fun so children an' everyone may enjoy themselves just a little more in these angelic ways of living.

I'm getting out of the pond, an' boy is this ground soft on my tootsies. I'm getting down under this lilac bush. Smells good. There is this most beautiful lion that keeps walking around. I am asking him to come an' lie down with me so I can use him as a cushy pillow. This golden beauty is coming over to me now. This furry delight is happy to have me as his friend. As we are lying down, I am resting my head on his belly so soft. It's fun to have my head move up an' down as he breathes. This lion is so perky an' full of joy. He will always be my friend. Any time I come back, he'll remember me.

I do know other lions that I have befriended in other parts of this land. An' I just really can't get enough of their friendship to suit me. So, I am always up for more. I love them. They tell me stories about their lives an' what they do an' how they feel.

My beauteous lion is telling me a story right now as I rest my head on his golden, soft hair. He has gone on many adventures in these ways of Light, an' some of his greatest joys are when birds tell him of their flights in the skies of Light, an' what they see, an' how it feels to fly, an' what they think about while they're flying in the thinking of angels. He said the birds sing together an' they ever so enjoy hearing each other's alive fun. They share back an' forth about the flowers they see, the love that courses through them as their wings flap. An' the speeds they get up to makes their bellies laugh. An' most of all the loving friendships they keep, an' the wonderful an' fun reunions with angelic people they get to attend an' be a part of.

I could listen to my lion's stories forever. They take me into my Light's sweetness. But things the lion likes more than almost anything is the laughter of children an' people's sparkles who come through these twinkly circlets for fun an' delight.

This lion joins in the golden circlets of life, greeting angels from other places far, far within. Places so deep in pools of purity that he has only to tell me that they are levels of life so filled in their shine of love that the kindness they release from themselves is especially enjoyable. An' these angelic ones bring with them streams of clean, scented, rainbow scintillating air.

My lion is living in sweet fun, an' he is always willing to share with visitors the fun that has been an' now is being given to him. He's telling me to always live in the aliveness of all of me because my life is always pulsing a love to all of life's circlets that are in me.

So as long as I stay in my Light's skilled self, I will always be Light. An' not only that, but I will be filled up with real joy every second of my foreverness. An' when this is happening, I get to be in the most loving places that my level of life can bring me.

I am loving this little lion friend of mine for sharing a little of his life with me. I'm telling him, "I love you." He's letting out a big roar as I am hugging him around his neck. His love is sweet.

I'm walking on this ever so soft grass, passing by the singing, playful water as it is splashing an' splashing with its ever so fun giggles. I'm reaching my little unicorn, an' up I go. She is glad to see me an' wants me to tell her all about my visit with the lion. She wants to know what the lion said.

So as it goes here in this Light paradise, every-thing mind chats with everything else. An' I love it this way. It's all good fun. Important angelic stuff.

I am taking off now to go for a fast speed ride through a rainbow swirl back into the white Light of life's many places of wonder. Talk about fun! Then after all this fun, I now am in a new land where new dancing love is beckoning me in to come an' play awhile.

I am getting a flash of a time with Daddy. We were sleeping outdoors in the mountains. I wanted to sleep by Daddy so much. So, he agreed. Which he never did. There were two pillows on a big blanket. I was about 4. Well, I loved marshmallows. Very seldom, we would get to roast them on our open fire. I hid a bunch of marshmallows under, I thought, my pillow to eat that night in secret. When I realized my marshmal-lows were under Daddy's pillow, I went to sleep.

Daddy was furious the next morning telling that a skunk stood on his chest an' would get a marshmal-low out from under his pillow, turn around on his chest to eat it as he wiggled his tail in Daddy's nose, then turn around an' get another marshmallow an' turn around on his chest again continuing to wiggle his tail each time in Daddy's face till the skunk ate every last one. Daddy said he had to use nerves of steel that long night. Boy is Daddy, as he says, "fit to be tied."

7

Sparkle by Sparkle

My miracle sweet unicorn an' I are going into new circlets of fun. There are several people that shine from the inside out here to greet me. Sweet love an' hugs are getting me to release a deep feeling like I am being tickled by these angels exciting ways of living.

Angelic wings are taking me to a very special place. I am leaving little unicorn here with the children so they can play with her. These angelic people wrap me up in soft love so I can be off to a beauteous world. I'm seeing Light sparks up ahead.

Oh my. This place is fabulously alive. It is all lit up an' has moving colors an' many swirls opening an' closing in rings of multiple colors.

This place is alive with access to all angelic realms. It is visited through these colorful rings by Light people that come from deep witnin themselves, a love place so deep that life breathes kindness into this space from a place of always love. This love is very active. Even the circlets talk an' have enlightenment in ways that this place completes itself by itself.

These people that live this entire place know how to release it out of themselves an' let it form their lives. When I got here, they knew that I too know the usage of my life an' my beginnings of life's forever that I am living from. Living insights have shown me what I'm made of an' how I am everything necessary to be able to be this level of inner usage of myself.

I am in this place now. Surrounding me is precious mind jewels that are made into shiny ways that are releasing tunes of welcome. Every sparkle of this jeweled paradise is sharing life's miracles. I am seeing two angelic people approaching. I feel their love strong.

"Hi."

"Hi, Kathy. We are so happy you came. There are a couple of things we do to stay alive in Light. One is we feel Light's happiness, an' another is we enjoy our ways of living in the sparkles."

I love being with angelic people. They have such easy ways about them. I feel welcomed as they are sharing with me the way their life lives itself. They are so actively pretty. Such joy looking into their sparkling, deep pools of love that is shining in their softness.

It's interesting seeing their inner an' outer bodies change colors in the same moments their Light thinking releases into their space of living. This entire world swirls out of these people's inner living.

This realness of them being the very place itself brings love, tears, an' joy to my colors within me. I see an' feel the way life is made an' lived an' enjoyed in the way life lives itself in its natural ways of being. I'm feeling their gentle love an' kindness for me. They smile as they hear my thinking an' excitement about being with them. I can tell they love having me here.

"Life works with life, Kathy. Living the life of a simple smile is you being life. Your life is springing forth the colors to make all things happen for you. We are making this place of Light by knowing Light. We are always living our forever Light life. We are ever forming our lives into more of life's surprises into life. Your joy of being in our liquid Light brings us close to you, Kathy. Light touches Light, so always be your Light.

"If you are thinking kindness, know that you put this kindness together sparkle by sparkle in a simple way. If you find yourself radiating outwardly from yourself Light rays, know it is you that is the Light you sparkle. It's your Light's nectar.

"Being the scent of a flower is you living an' being you. Also, you shining your sunlight of your own warmth is you being sun.

"We are blossoming ourselves out of our glowing orb. As we are using the love an' Light of our very own jewels, we are living life inwardly an' outwardly, blossoming into beautiful places where our body form does glow like sparkling angels. Our bodies are always making themselves out of our forever life.

"As we become more useful to ourselves, we begin to know we are all things in us an' around us. Then this living naturally blossoms forth as our precious selves live on. We are making many attachments within ourselves as we continue being Light, Kathy. Life is always forming us into purity Light if we let it.

"This is done in a place that puts together form. We call this place a visible body. So always know that in your own self is your only Light stabilizer point you have that does form you into an angelic person. With you, you have you blossoming yourself. Care for your body, for it is your everything. It is your skilled, angelic

Light body as well as your unskilled, earthly, so-called fleshly Light body. They are one an' the same. So, circle yourself into skilled Light an' live the miracle way.

"You are the inner Light colors that are opening inside of you. You are the wellsprings of colors that bring forth your life. You are all the sparkles that you turn into form. All sparkles of you are all life that you will ever have to use an' reuse.

"We are always pulsing deeper into our Light self. That's how I am here in this miracle land that you feel an' see all around you, Kathy. It's because Light is our life being lived in ways of self that can only be activated through the Light usage of one's own self. An' now we must take our leave."

Such love an' graciousness as these activated-in-Light angels are walking away. They are looking back an' Light thinking, "What a nice piece of life." This piece of life they are Light thinking about is me. I have a warm an' cozy feeling inside.

The glowing angelic ones that carried me here are here now, wrapping me inside their sparkling angel arms that are cozy an' ever so soft. An' within moments I am looking back at this so joyous place. How simple it is, using one's own Light to blossom one's home an' life out of.

My angelic friends place me on my diamond saddle that glistens in life's purities. I twinkle the Light people with my love, an' off little unicorn an' I go through another swirl of life's white Light into our now self once more.

8

Rainbow Wings

My swirling in the circlets of rainbows is very active. I feel something new in me. I am being released from this rainbow of love into a Light realm filled with angel music. This place is touching me deeply. These sounds travel like sunshine. I begin to sit down an' then lie down by the brook of soft, sparkling water.

As I'm hearing the flowing water passing over the ruby, sapphire, an' opal stones, I'm entering into a deep sleep an' awakening into a land where angelic people are telling me many miracle things about this new form I am now going to be enjoying.

The swirls of rainbow Light left me a whole person, so no longer always having to use my little unicorn unless I choose to enjoy her for a fun ride.

My angelic friends are saying, "Kathy, you look more like us now with your circlets of Light flowing an' swirling within you an' around you like wings that are releasing Light movement bringing you more angelic freedom. Also, you can instantly be wherever you like. This joining of yourself is a most exciting time for you.

"When you awaken into the land of music again, Kathy, remember all we are saying here an' all you are seeing here. An' remember, you look like us an' have awakened many angelic seeds in you that we have awakened in us. We will be getting together with you many times to acquaint you with your fun new colors. These star sparks carry you into miracle roads.

"These are new skills so you can go into many new places within you. We will be right there with you. We are your angel Light family. We love you an' are very excited for you."

As I awaken, I look around at the streams of love flowing over the jewels. Never on Earth have I seen such beautiful water an' rocks. Yet here, everything takes on a new, fresh, shiny, clear radiance similar to looking into a star. That's why I call these places miracles.

As I'm seeing the fairies in their multicolored selves flying an' landing an' ever so enjoying themselves, I too feel the delight that's happening inside these happy ways we live within ourselves. This is another way of us having fun in life's many forms.

I am so tickled to be here, yet I am remembering what the angelic ones are saying as I am sleeping by the brook. They are saying to me that I look like them now. What exactly do they mean? I'm looking around for little unicorn. I love her so much.

As I'm getting up, looking around, an' realizing what's been happening in these circlets of rainbow Lights as these angelic ones are putting me on my sparkling diamond saddle as we, little unicorn' an' I, begin swirling around in white sparkling spirals as we're journeying into our next adventure.

Oh my. I'm feeling the changes that are taking place within us. Little unicorn's abilities are joining in mine. I get to enjoy having instant travel with instant arrival through myself to go anywhere in using my Light travel as my way of getting around without me being little unicorn. Yes, it's me. We are our everything.

Well, if I don't call this miraculous, I don't know what is. Oh my goodness! This is why the angelic people are telling me I look like them. They are gently awakening me softly an' slowly into my new changes so it will come as a pleasant surprise for me.

"Oh my," I say to myself as I am seeing my outer forms sparkling in angelic, swirling, colorful streamers that are forming me into looking like delicate, precious shapes like it is in these angelic ones I'm seeing while asleep by the brook. I'm looking like I have wings.

What in Life have I become? Oh my. As I sit back down by this glowing hillside that is glistening in rays of soft green, yellow, an' pink, I lean up against this hill that is all aglow an' begin feeling the love sparkles tickling my back as I'm pondering over these many changes in me.

I do not want to leave here, but I know I must because my life in earthly ways is writing all this down an' I must join this part of me to get my day going.

So, back in my visible self, an' life picks up as always. No one is aware of my new fun ways of living, yet people are treating me differently with more smiles an' some people are asking me about the Light they see around me.

Some say to me that I am an angelic Light sent to Earth to cheer people up. I say I am paying attention to our Light's life within us as our angelic hugging an' thinking does reach into each other's worlds.

9

Diamond Rowboat

I am anxious to see where I end up in my new ways of getting places instantly. This is going to take some getting used to. A place of peace is my quest.

I find myself in a rowboat that is made out of angelic, loving thinking. My new colors that are looking like wings circle out an' into me allowing my little Lightself to form this little rowboat. I am relaxing into an afternoon of floating on the ripples an' waves.

I got to thinking about the water under me. An' looking over the sides of my lovely little boat, I am seeing entire places formed in this water. How can this be? Pathways where people are walking, gliding along. What is this place? I've never seen such a place in water. What am I to do here? I feel like stepping into this water as if there are paths that will hold me, an' I know there are. A funny feeling, I have, but I'm going to do it. Stepping out of my sparkling rowboat right out into the water, I begin to sink through the liquid right onto a golden pathway down a steep incline.

The watery substance is not wet like water. It's made out of a life substance that releases out of people's lives. People's life nectar is what makes everything in the Light worlds live.

My self is aglow with twinkling feelings that are sparkling fun for me. I'm swirling in golden Light as I am guided by glittery sparkles coming out of jeweled butterflies. They are taking me into an' through a high, arched golden tunnel. As I am passing through, there is a pinging sound as the gold sparks a diamond shine throughout this enormous, golden dome.

I am approaching a central, golden, massive human Flame. It's an intense feeling that brings tears to my eyes of what the significance of this place is doing. Love's skills are being given to people that are lost in their own blossoming of self. Never before have I known or felt anything so revealing in the pure basics of the twisted ways an' usage of our lives. An' never have I ever felt the beauty of life's ways so strongly.

I'm seeing colorful angels coming an' going in continuous streams, releasing into the flame from their very selves a nectar so pure that it scarcely seems that real people could have in them so much skillful living action in a usable substance for their own lives, an' are choosing to share with us much of this substance.

I am so glad life is always bringing us into our Light. This is so overwhelming that life is like this. That angel people are able to share with us like this is so perfect, an' ever so real, that we get the care to survive the depths of our change in us. I am so quickly awakened. All I can say right now is I am vibrating in the love tears for all of us.

These angels are thickly layered out of Light. Their outer an' inner body layers are solid an' set in place. They have become untouchable by any outside force. They are inwardly protected, potent Light forms that are releasing internal substances in its purest form for the finest usages of mankind's most necessary join-ings. This Light is given to people so they can survive in Light ways. This personalized nectar brings awaken-ing miracle ways into people.

These angelic people assist us in being able to continue our lives in the most challenging circumstanc-es. These angels give of their personal life, their own life's nectar. They give up some of their personal self an' usage of self to feed others. They give of their own inner life's food. Their naturally sustaining substances are given to us for our survival of our life that keeps our life going. Diamond angels are choosing to share.

These are the things that are being communi-cated to me at this moment. I am actually in the presence of these purity people. All life benefits from these people's giving. I am aware that it takes real people with real lives giving us real nectar from their real, alive lifeline. This Light nectar can get our life roll-ing in the Light ways. We are the ingredients of life.

Nevertheless, these angels an' other inner-exchanging angelic personalities are releasing a con-stant golden-diamond orb out of their sensitive, jeweled, softly put together Light body an' souls' nectar is surging into this flame delicious love. This is an out-pouring of personal Light. The most precious, valued substance in their lives is divvied out to us that can use a droplet. Every drop they can spare. These angels an' people like them have been doing this since visible ways of living in unskilled form beckoned their love.

Love is great coming to us out of them, internally feeding us precious life from their bodies so that their personal blossoming has been, to a degree, changed for them till each one of us are returned to our skilled place of making our own life's current an' become once again drawing on our own nectar's function of usage for our daily sustenance as it is intended for us to do. Angels' lives are assisting us into our angel ways.

I must close. The vibrant life that is moving my pen on Earth is waning. I am entering the archways an' looking back into where the angelic people are circling this golden, living flame. Diamond angels come, release their nectar into the flame an' go quickly.

These beautiful beings that are perfected people are diametrically opposed opposites from the people that are these flames. Sharing angels bringing Light in this space is bringing about a turning around a person's attaching into a person's Light. As these diametrically opposed lifestyles are joining together in this space of reversal, Light shares an' joins into a Light infusing friendship for these people. This is a roaring life flame that only protectors of Light can get close enough to.

As I am being made aware that this flame is the very lives of countless unskilled living people, these people that are in this liquid form of the flame are trying to contain an' manage their own life's dynamic miracle love. Our heavenly inheritance. So these protector angels are coming from skilled Light ways of living to take turns in containing these people until the people themselves can get functional in their own usage of self in the angelic an' unskilled ways they exist.

These purity ones cannot let me too close to the center of this roaring human life fame. The room feels extremely tense, yet love is in the extremes.

10

The Nectar of the Elves' Golden Goblet

As a little girl of 7, I am thinking about babies in bellies when I hear in my thinking, "A baby will blossom on its own in our tummies when it is ready." I think I see little round eggs in me awaiting to spring fourth. Wow!

My life's rainbow swirl is releasing me an' my little unicorn by a very large golden goblet. Its golden shine is crystal-like an' special to look at. This place talks to everyone about the life nectar that brings forth life. There are no teachers here. I am receiving information directly from the place itself.

I am aware of the internal purpose of the life's properties that make up life itself. I am being given a clarity that I am now writing about.

This place is its own maker. Its function permeates anyone that gets close to it. Having an internal desire to know about life's function does draw people to this place, an' these insights into life will be instilled into the one inquiring about such things.

Light nectar is the stimulus for the birth of an egg. When there is enough nectar in a person the egg will be penetrated by its aliveness, an' naturally, an' in the natural timing, bring life forth.

Light nectar does not only bring a woman's egg to birth a child all by itself, but also feeds the human bodies of male an' female, feeding the brain, mind, an' bodies in the skilled an' unskilled parts of ourselves. This Light's nectar is the inner life that creates the outer formed us an' also brings us complete nutrition out of, through, an' into our outer bodies.

When an egg awakens in its own natural time, this child that is the egg will come into existence prepared an' equipped in its blossoming of its inner centers. An' with one's inner attachments, there is an abundance of nectar in the person to draw on for life's many movements in the miracle ways life lives itself.

Some people question, "Am I a boy or a girl?" A person's journey in their forever living continuously brings about a person's form. Each one's personal usage of this nectar determines the way a person is formed. We are being fed this Light nectar into our inner Light self. This is what keeps our pretty self-regenerating out of the multifunctional reinventing abilities of our Light worlds that we are blossoming out of.

We are always bringing ourselves into a balance. Boy an' girl being in one self brings about birthing from one's own lifeforce all through one person. An unskilled body is an unfed Light self that is bringing out of our life many ways that are not in a miracle direction.

When our birthing has plenty of Light nectar, then this beautiful joining of ourselves forever is birthing us an' life flourishes for us into a Light way of birthing in us. We are relying on our self to birth us into only Light ways of living our personalized foreverness. Life is relying on itself in each of us. This is boy-girl.

I'm seeing my colors changing as I feel this place releasing me from its grip. This place is leaving its message in me as I am writing it down in my book on Earth. I am free to go.

This place is a joy to visit. I am on my unicorn, ready to enter the swirl of Love once more. The message is alive in me. This all is wonderful for my book.

But now that I am here, I am asking if I could just stay an' look around a bit in the gardens, an' I am getting permission. This is so nice. I am riding my little unicorn under the waterfalls an' through the lush gardens. The moisture is delightful. The waterfalls are like a liquid, clear blue color flowing over me. It's real soft. I am so happy to have been let in to play in this place. The tropical sounds are like a singsong melody.

I am getting off my little unicorn to walk in this clear stream of refreshing water. I'm coming up upon a bunch of elves. This is my first time ever seeing any. What a sight. They seem to be expecting me. Wow! What fun! I would so like to see everyone from Earth enjoying this place. Let's sit down with the elves on the side of the brook. As we're sitting, I'm so excited with all this joyous singing an' dancing.

The fun of it all is feeling so automatic that little unicorn an' I are joining into the fun flying, spinning, an' playing in the chase, twirling at quick speeds, rolling backwards, forwards, landing in colorful, soft lily ponds giggling till our little hearts blossom into sparkles.

Each Light person is special. No matter who I come across in Light travels, I feel something new.

It's so nice that life has so many places I can visit an' take part in. I do tell more of a difference in people here than on Earth. It's the vast differences in the usage of one's Light nectar that brings about a myriad of changes in unexplainable ways of one's Light self. I so enjoy being in the fun of these new things. It's something I take with me each time. They all are cumulative. Sparkles make my Earth life much easier to use.

I am blossoming into new places all the time. Traveling inwardly brings fun like an enjoyable vacation. The interaction with the people is as sweet as a fun hug. It's just people with different skills of living. An' for these people, Light usage is the way here.

Everyone is happy to talk about their travels into Light realms where angelic people live, an' is much talk about how we become so many different angelic colors. It's popular to shine one's love here. Love is the prized possession, along with kindness an' the ability to be free in Light.

These people are saying they use all of their nectar to improve their usage of life an' are proud to do it. It's the reason to live here. Everyone is allowing themselves to be the Lighted people that they are.

I feel my time with the elves is over. I'm beginning to drift away. Little unicorn an' I are riding through the streams. An' as I am passing the golden goblet, I can hear the thinking of the elves an' feel their love an' happiness for our visit, an' I can feel the joy they're feeling for us having our new found friends an' Light travel fun. Me an' little unicorn are so happy.

Through the rainbow swirl we go. I am filled with much love for these elves. I've become so attached in such a short time. So fun they are, an' open with a welcoming joy. I get to always feel their life's love in me.

11

A Shiny, Pearly Glow

Our sun that we see in the sky is us, our nectar, an' our life's juice. Our sun warms us all an' feeds us life-giving sustenance. The living glow of us is the sun. We can see ourselves in the moon, in the rays of sunlight. Our food is always there for us. It's always with us, feeding us real, welcomed Light into ourselves.

We are comforted by the sparkle of our lives being sunlight. We are baby suns. We give off Light as our eyes shine sunny rays out of them. We do send shafts of Light rays out of our hands. We are loving ourselves from a distance, an' sharing our rays with each other an' through all of nature.

I am glad to know that the rays an' cleansing sun is coming from us. We reach for the nipple of Light to nurture us. We use the bright Light to cling to. We get sunny hugs to bring us a joyous feeling. Looking into the sun upon awakening, it's all there for us. We have this place in us an' outside of us to use as we join into looking in an' soaking up sun before sleep. Sweet!

This sun is so necessary for an angelic Light baby birthed out of Light. This Light reality is guiding us, nurturing us. Being sun gives us the ability to birth our forever lives. An' as you can see, the sun is our simple example of its heavenly ways, giving of self freely. glowing in purity's beauty, an' releasing itself into all of us so we have what is ours to use.

At the core of our lives is the life of the sun. It's what we are made out of. It's our life itself. With the sun shining into our lives, we are fed the finest food from synthesizing flora an' fauna through a living process known only to the body. We are alive because of this way our body has skills, just as our bodies have skills to feed a baby an' birth a baby. There is a lot to us.

We are receiving our inner nectar because of the sun in us an' outside of us. We are enjoying the nectar releasing its life out of plants an' animals in alive ways their life lives itself. These are ways angels an' we are fed from living things only. We are already sipping the same as angels sip. I am so glad to know.

We know in our deepest Light of our self what it's like to live with all things provided for us. It's us being happy with the ways we are provided for. Life is on the inside of us providing for all of us, an' always will. Life has not changed. We have.

As a kid, an' now in my life, eating, an' drinking water or any other liquid, is an' has been a very small part of my day. Some days liquids an' solids are not in my day at all. My nectar automatically feeds an' waters me. Knowing this relaxes me an' brings me another touch of my freedom. I am alive an' fed because of the way miracle life lives itself. An' we are all fed in the same ways. We are alive because of Light food.

What a miracle we are, being the fountain of our food that springs up from within us. This is the way the angels are fed, an' so are we.

12

I Ask Myself

I'm asking myself to help me to align my jaw, an' within a few seconds I'm feeling a strong, intense strength on both sides of my face an' my jaw is aligning. Wow. I know it can happen, an' it does. In thirty seconds.

I'm on a date. I need to pay for food so our date cannot be girlfriend. No money. I wish with all my being... Looking. A crisp $5.00 bill is in my wallet. Wow.

I'm wiggling out of my inner tube, rolling under an' under, seeing Daddy's legs, thinking why is Daddy not pulling me up. Angels pull me up. Daddy grabs me.

For a few years my eyes would just drip when I would try to read. Hurt so bad. Extreme blur. I'm telling myself that I will read. An' within six weeks I'm reading small print. My eyes are soft an' feeling happy.

I'm on a winding mountain road. I cannot get my snow chains on. I'd like help, I was thinking. A man that looks a bit shiny appears an' begins putting my chains on, never saying a word, an' vanishes.

I'm half way with 75 miles to go, gas gauge below empty. An orange ball of Light came out of me an' it travels into my gas tank. I make it all the way.

I'm using fun purity thinking as my Light touches my angelic self in my active place where I sparkle with life inside me.

13

Dashing Through the Light

Visiting a friend thousands of miles away, or in Heaven, an' going places through my love swirls of myself, I do slip me an' my Light self so easily into the fun adventure I am pulsing into. An' the real doing of the thing is really being done.

Let's say you want to give your mom a kiss on the cheek an' a big hug, but she is not there with you. Or maybe she is in Heaven, or lives a long way away. You can slip through your love swirl, an' with your Light functions give your mom the biggest hug an' kiss ever. She will feel it in some part of her, an' so will you. Life is constant in its access to each other.

I'm glad you're reading my book. This book came out of my forever life livec by me. It would be a loving, sharing moment to read an online book review, a little something from your sparkle of life. If I could get a few droplets of Light from each one that reads my book, it will be sweet fun for me.

Little unicorn an' I are feeling rainbow sparkles of love, an' I know your beautiful Light self is touching mine as you an' I are continuing to bring our inner Light self out of us into angelic form.

14

Jewels Are Angels' Minds

I'm visiting an angel. We're talking. She's saying, "When you come to my home, Kathy, you see my seeds in me blossoming into everything you see.

"We all have our own Light seeds. This is what makes us personalized. I am the angelic tree. I am the glittery waterfall. I am the glowing walkways. I am the sparkling home you're seeing all around me. It's just the same for you on Earth. You are everything around you just as I am. We are, within ourselves, all things.

"The part of me that is my sun is separate from yours. But when our suns mix together, they shine a mighty sun in the sky. An' when my air comes together with your air, mighty winds or gentle winds can be the outcome. Each of us is joined, yet separate.

"Our droplets of water, when they are joined, make for mighty oceans an' gentle streams. When our self becomes jeweled, we are seen by each other. Until then, we are misty Light. What is Heaven, you ask? It's you. Heaven is someplace we are made into, an' someplace we are made out of.

"Sweet little Kathy, we're all living in the same place an' ways. You're a humming bird on Earth. Those are the same humming birds you are in Heaven.

"Earth an' Heaven are the same place. Sweet Kathy, becoming aware of yourself is what you are doing. You see, you are the life that makes up the moon, stars, flowers, trees, laughter, an' happy ways.

"All of life is lived in Heaven as it is lived on Earth. We are one an' the same place. What is within you is also outside of you.

"You say, Kathy, that we Light people look like jeweled prisms, multicolored shining orbs. Well, so do all of you on Earth. You see, our angelic bodies are the jewels you see an' have on your Earth.

"Our lives shape an' reshape all things we are to suit our ways at the time. This is the way life lives, Kathy. The gold, crystals, an' diamonds of your world are our very selves. They are living parts of our Light self. We use these parts of ourselves in our thinking to form our world an' way of life out of. An' you also are these jewels. They are the very brain an' mind of us all.

"Our life is forming an' then reforming. You do not live in a separate world from ours. We are drawing on our earthly selves just as you all are.

'It is best to leave the precious jewels an' all sparkling, living substances alone in their place of living so we can access our living, undisturbed parts of our lives from all these levels of ourselves.

"Our inner jewels bring us jeweled form for the purposes of completing ourselves. We are drawing on an' forming ourselves out of an' into the ways miracles function. This is where everything is allowed to live.

"Your visits are fun for me Kathy," my angel says as she enfolds me in her loving wings. An' as I feel her releasing me, she then sparkles off.

15

A Light Being's Jewels

My angelic friend is my special gift from life. Being in touch with our angelic self is being alive an' filled up with a happy reality. My life takes on a glow of happiness, an' I'm freshening up with special moments my Light self shares with me.

Our angelic friends are our living angel relatives an' our family of Light that is assisting in our ability to use life. Our angel's Light attaching ways are our true examples of how to conduct ourselves in our living process. By example, they assist us in our daily living. The depth of their love brings us into thinking clearly. Their skills activate ours in a simple sharing.

It is best for us to know that as we rely on our precious stones, gold, silver, crystals, plants, animals, an' air along with all life that we are, we will flourish an' prosper only from all things in their alive ways. As are Light self will only use gold, silver, crystals, animals, plants, an' every living thing through an internal, attaching, alive usage. These are our worlds where we live in our Light part of us. We are chipping away at our angel homes of alive usage in our Light body's connection to them. Death in us is when our life is removed from its inner natural ways of staying alive.

By us receiving inner-body food an' water, we, being self-sufficient, relinquishes our need to rely on living things in the devouring way we use them for our means of survival leaving gold, silver, jewels, crystals, animals, an' plants to continue their part in being life so that our Light self can continue a forever life in this living, attached, natural way we an 'angels survive.

Whirling in the angelic forever way is within our grasp. Living a living life comes from our beginnings. We have forever to bring ourself back to a proper way.

An' being guided by angelic friends is a way of listening. To listen to the living, one has to rely on their own skills to make inner sharing happen. It's a twofold process. They have what we have, sweet life to go inwardly, so we must rely on our alive ways to go inward. Angelic ones live only in the living. An' that's where we do come from. So the only place we can get an angelic friend is in the place they live. An' that's through attached access to our own living abilities.

We can have living conversations with our special friends. Angelic ones are a living attachment an' feeling away. We will get the hang of it. Alive travel is a wonderful thing. It opens up our ways of living in the Light. The heavens are inside of us an' are outside of us. Taking this literally changes us.

The sweet journey is taken with our inner-outer mind in jeweled activity with itself. Our Light bodies are proliferating jewels. Reach ever deeper into our angelic self. We are there, an' always have been. It is a little more fun as our desire picks up for this kind of life. It's good to know we can share with angels an' go far.

16

Crystal Road

I like sparkling with places of Light within me as I'm riding my little unicorn into these angel joys. As we're galloping further into the center of these beauties, these crystal roads are leading us into angelic nectar that is releasing freedoms only happy ways can bring. I'm seeing Light people arriving.

The skies are filled with glowing fun colors as these Light people appear in them. Everything is lit up in a dance of soft love. Yet, I am seeing more an' more angels. Streams of love are pouring in from outlying Lighted worlds from far, far within each of these especially refined people. I am glowing in fun sparkles. We are in the middle of love sharing. Yay!

I'm getting off little unicorn an' leaving her in a field of playful unicorns. Being among the many angelic people is much joy for me. I'm entering the very fancy Light. Sweet birds, puppies, an' fairies are loving me. This is our home of liquid silver, our beginnings of forming into misty Light.

Our lives are our sweetness springing up into these vibrant, happy, colorful bubbles of glowing Light. I'm feeling refreshing tingles as I'm moving through an' going deeper into this active place.

Cherubs an' such beauteous people are releasing me into these innermost circlets of glowing pools of living Light swirling around me as I am joining these ethereal, shiny jewels swirling in beautiful orbs.

From this feeling in me, I am in another one of life's ways for joy an' Light action sharing into one's life as it brings reversal back to being only skilled Light. All is in Light thinking in these celebrations. Ever so much love is made an' given out for people that are holding an' bringing their lives an' ways of living into purity.

This is a massive gathering of diamond shiny angels that are bringing us sensitive reviving streamers that activate our Light centers. The love people with all their Light are wrapping us in their kindness as we're using special Light functions in their presence of sharing wondrous ways. These influences are stimulation for us to be able to know ourselves an' to activate our ways of living that rely only on an alive ecosystem from every way of surviving. What a joy to know life is bringing life into us through the usage of life's skill of sharing life's necessities while being alive. Yahoo!

This place is sending out love beams, soft an' gentle rays, into me. I am responding giddily to this beauty. I feel this loving Light entering me. This precious nectar coming from these angelic ones are springing clearer thinking into the very workings of each of us, dissolving how we became not properly used Light.

These strands of loving, active influence releases out of the lives of these evolved, heavenly occupants. This all is miracle internal skills an' internal assistance being released directly into our lives. What a sweet way as we are becoming more of our Light. All life receives gentle sparkles from these perfected ones. The cherub people in all this precious Light are bringing me out as they fly with me. I love them so much.

I'm here now with my little unicorn friend, hopping up on her back, an' off we're going through the rainbow Light. These enjoyments an' benefits are oceans of internal gifts.

Remember, everyone swirling with their purity attaching into beautiful ways of thinking does enjoy special love. Are we all using love to reach into our Light worlds to pulse inwards our unskilled thinking into life's freedoms? Yes, we do use much love.

"Bye bye," I wave to a few angelic ones as little unicorn an' I whisk away.

We can see angels. Yes, we can. Glowing angels are being seen by us as we look into the sun. Angels' outer part of them is so bright an' beautifully perfected that the heavens that they live in shines their presence right through an' into our world. Angels an' we are glowing sunlight.

The purpose of our forming into this next step of becoming form is so our misty ways can bring about a quick touching into a contact that congeals our Light sparkles in a joining that gives us an angelic outer frame. This gives us our Light traveling capabilities. Our body form is intended to bring our misty form into a way of forever Light travel. This is our body's purpose.

My brother is a new arrival in Heaven. He has a wonderful message: "I am deeply aware of how calm love is the solution to problems. If only I had used this." I'm so glad my brother knows now that love has skills.

17

Be Skilled Light Forever

Little unicorn an' I are prancing around an' being coddled in soft thoughts. We begin seeing a lovely Light
person approaching us.

It's always so special being around a person that
lives in these levels of Light. I can feel myself glowing
in sweet love as I am climbing down off of my little unicorn's diamond saddle.

This place is the reminders of life's ways that
brings completion to our birth of being skilled Light.

A lot of what's going on in me is I'm seeing in a
circular way all around me. I am being surrounded in
my mind an' skilled Light body with places that are
trickling into my vision from my yellow rose angel's
view of ife. I like this way of seeing.

Angels' minds that are their skilled Light bodies
have it really nice. Angelic ones are passing Light information into me. This is a way of bringing me into
their world. This is a way of being heard an' cared
about. I am being tickled with star sparkles. These star
sparkles come out of pretty thinking.

"Life is simple, Kathy. It's all about making us into a Light self that includes a skilled Light body so we
can bring ourselves into our joining with everything

alive. Our way of life then stays protected and stays this way forever. Our alive Light body is the very reason we have angelic travel. We are the signal that sparks the signal to activate our heavenly movement.

"In a body with no living skills, we become what's making up earthly nature just like our vibrant, Light-skilled ways are what's making us into angels an' all heavenly ways in us. As we're having no living skills, we're entering into decomposing. We do not hold up the same as we do when we are using living ways, yet we keep going an' nevertheless still exist.

"A no-Light life births itself into many no Light ways. Skilled Light ways gets to be our freedom, our one an' only way we're supposed to live.

"A living body that is not properly used is what we call an earthly body. Or we call it an undeveloped Light person. You see, in the living there's no choice or death. Choice is nothing more than an angel willing to assist us in becoming our skilled, living self.

"Being our miracle self needs no choice. Being miracles brings no needs. Being life in miracles is freedom in always knowing to blossom ourselves out of happy living things. No choice is needed in alive ways. Only activation in the living brings us our ever-continuing Light birthing. This is what we call 'Heaven.'"

My angel is taking me on some tours, an' is saying to all of us that our precious lives touch her joy. So if you like, you can travel here in your sleep, or from your Light home, an' have a little fun with your skilled ways of becoming your forever-Lighted you.

18
Rising Light (Part 1)

After I finish writing my book, I talk to my angels to find out what's up with the fallen person that is known to be an angel that is written about in our history. My angels give me the go ahead an' is letting me write this true account of explaining the way life falls an' rises. Rising Light is bringing this message from life so we can read with our angelic-attaching angel skills as we go into life's ways. An' so, here we go.

I like sparkling in these glowing swirls of Light within my mind, an' riding my little unicorn which adds much fun an' adventure to my visits with the Lighted ways of life. I am mounting my little unicorn. Off we go through the night sky.

We begin entering into pinpoints of multicolored Lights. As we're galloping further into this glow, it begins opening into an entire city of exquisite living.

Angels are arriving in an array of rainbow droplets pulsing through levels of love coming from their Lighted homes from deep within themselves.

These places are pulsing with people's sharing purities releasing freedoms that only live ways can bring about. These angels are arriving in droves. This abundance of inner contacts to developed angels is so lovely. These skies they are entering through are as beautifully adorned in colors as the angels themselves. These attachings to love angels continues to glow above, below, an' on the sides of me. These orbs of angels' Light is lit in a glow of soft, golden, pulsing love.

As far as I can see below me, above me, an' on the sides of me is living ways of life so very colorful an' alive. Yet I see more an' more levels of Light people chiming into this event streams of love pouring in from blossoming Light worlds from where our lives live from far, far within us where beauteous angels an' beings are glistening in continuous jewels coming out of Heaven's heart.

This is a special occasion. I'm getting off my little unicorn an' leaving her by a silvery trough. I am wandering among the many people of Light. They are captivating me with the usage of their Love.

As I enter these angel creations, many birds an' lions are greeting me. This place is glowing its shiny, happy love. It's alive like a brisk dip in the ocean.

My everything enjoys penetrations from this dancing love radiating out of these vibrant walls. It's fun for me as I am feeling these angels swirling themselves into this angelic event. I'm so happy as I am being caringly loved in a joyous freedom. It feels like being gobbled up in hugs of love dissolving everything other than miracle ways. I am wishing my words will bring visuals to you of the beauty of this place. I am going into the innermost diamond chambers. There are pools of dancing fountains everywhere. This thick crystal is compounded in jewels, intense, gorgeous feelings of goodness an' extreme caring in entire worlds of angels.

As I am writing this all down on paper in my Earth body, I am doing my best to stay awake. Being in so much flowing ways of angelic food entering into me droplets of sparkling nutrition does soothe me an' comfort me in feelings of sweetness.

I am being seated by some lovely flying angel fairies. They're fun an' ever so pretty all at the same time. From the insight from within myself, from the buzz in the courtyard, this is another one of this fallen one's returning to Light's blossoming moments. There have been many. Much assistance is given to this one. This fallen one has been pulsing itself into the places of Light within, trying to use its skills in rising Light.

Everyone here is pushing for this one to use its golden thread in the Light once an' for all. There is a massive gathering of the most stupendously skilled angels in attendance. There are these uplifting, Light-infusing, reviving moments going on in a continuous way from the moment of this fallen one's mishap with the inner attachings of itself. These attachings are necessary to blossom our Light lives.

This fallen one is struggling using the activating points in itself. It's a road of success, eventually, for all of us. Living the life of ourselves is easily done in the Light. As long as one uses life in the Light, then life is easy an' fun in an automatic, natural way.

It's the same as anything that is living. All things in it has everything within its reach to survive. Like a tree, the dirt is just there. It is natural an' easy. A fish in the water just swims in the water. The water is just there for the fish's life to be complete. We Light people live in Light. That's where we all are born an' blossom.

The angels love this one with all their Light, an' are wrapping this fallen person in their skills of sharing their Light that they have become in their own selves. Their influence is giving this fallen one reviving access to Light areas within itself.

It's the way we use ourselves that brings what happens to us. The self is the place all life begins from. This is all any of us can do, an' that's to be the Light of ourselves that we are meant to be. What a comfort to know angels are sharing with, an' giving to, each of us. Life is so good when we use it right.

I am in an array of rainbow love. Above me an' below me is soft Love beams of penetrating, kind, an' gentle rays. I am sweetly quivering in this aliveness. Angels of all levels of life are touching us with pure angelic joy that is bringing us a feeling of "It's okay."

This fallen one is coming into this precious, skilled Light an' is being surrounded in very large protector angels that are releasing circlets to all these countless angels. Protector angels release bands of Light to strengthen angels safety. These are angels that are endlessly attaching an' always blossoming into entire Light existences, continuously living in forever, sparkling worlds surrounded in layer after layer of lifeforce that does keep one's purity protected.

Delicate love that is releasing an' weaving its Light food as it is deeply infusing angel love into themselves as this love is traveling also into all Light spectrums that the angels are caring about. Angels' compounded life juice of internal an' external ways of living in Light has turned these angels into what is known as a "love-shield angel" that protects Light.

These joinings of angels are releasing pure streams of angelic food. This sweet way of giving the life of Light is traveling into this fallen one as a miracle sharing. This swirling love is so precious. I can tell this one can use a lot of sharing from these friendly angels. This fallen one looks like a gold person. This fallen one has an earthly appearance an' looks like solid gold.

I am noticing the Light circlets are swirling out of these countless angels' pools of love swirling into this fallen one's life. A joyous tune, a soft melody, sweet music in this Light paradise. This person is beginning to loosen a solid appearance an' is taking on a wave like movement that brings this one caring ways.

This gathering is working miracles to bring real love to this one's lifeline. An' this fallen one is willing. What a miracle in progress. Life has beautiful ways to share with us. This sunshine of a place is a touch of Heaven. We are surely being remembered.

This rising Light is entering an' surrounding this person, an' this person is leaving without the skilled protector's Light intervening that is depended on to enter a transformative Light of angels' love. I am happy for the fallen one. So much life movement for all of us.

As our lives share in each other's angelic ways of nourishing ourselves, we too begin enjoying the angels' way of eating, living, an' having fun. This is all a wonderful new way for us all. Stepping into angels' worlds an' ways of sharing, our Light does twinkle us into purity's arms as we drink the beginnings of life into our skeletal, fleshly, jeweled self; our forever body.

19
Rising Light (Part 2)

As little unicorn an' I are enjoying the memories of our lovefest of angels' love sharing moments, we in a flash our journey takes a turn into a valley of roses. Sweet aromas are delighting our finest pleasures.

"What is this place?" I say to little unicorn as an angel appears in all her flowing Light garb that makes her spectacular to see.

What a treat, feeling the way one feels being around such precious life. I'm dancing in Love sharing. My eyes are glowing in pools of Light. I'm so happy as I climb down off of little unicorn an' glide into a place of wise ways of attaching life in forever living. This entire place is the depths of all of our minds. Todays, tomorrows, an' yesterdays. So nice it's here to know.

My quest for information is being granted. This angel's eyes shining in mine as she passes her desire into me on how to follow her is a way of being touched in knowings that uses no words. But I feel exactly what she is having me know. The movement of her love is so fun. I feel like she enjoys me an' is finding her sharing with me fun for her too.

It's a delight as I'm liked. It feels so sweet. I really like people that are living in heavenly miracle ways.

This twinkling person is leaving me here to take in what it is that is needed by me. I am left alone in this place that has diamonds as decorations around just about everything. I am being made aware that these diamonds are our life's inner way of mind travel.

Our mind, skull, an' all of our framework is blossomed into an' are layered in crystalline Light levels. In every way, we are these jeweled parts of us in places of Light that are blossoming within us. Wow. We're beautifully put together.

This fallen one that is known to be an angel is my quest to see what went on an' is going on with this one an' why did whatever happen cause so much furor down through the ages an' still does.

An' I would also like to know what causes other people to change out of heavenly living. I am writing all this down with pen an' paper on Earth in my physical body level as I am receiving from my Light-body level.

Sitting with these diamonds an' hearing their messages speaking to my innermost self is exciting for me. This information is flowing into me. So here we go.

"We people are raised in Light, an' the only way we know to live is in the Light. When the fallen one's rising Light stops using itself in any way, its Light can thrive. Then unhappy becomes alive.

"Our lives being lived always in ways that brings us into miracles is why we stay in a blossoming circle. This brings us into a way of being angels. Until this level is reached, one gets very close before one becomes on the inside of them an' the outside of them, in a continuous way, Light's pretty, glowing love. It's permanent once we complete our joining into angelic, alive ways.

"This fallen person is one that reaches all but the doing of such a level of its life. An' there is one sparkle of self left for this one to blossom into itself before swirling up this one's entire being into the everlasting arms of itself becoming an angel. So this fallen one automatically begins using its leaking Light food in a way that starts this person on a path into another way, an' takes a terrible tumbling fall into misuse of the way life an' mind functions from self in Light. An' this is the turning of events that this one is bringing back the skill of Light attaching. Its ever so long ago that this began, Kathy."

"Sweet Light, thank you for giving me all this I have been seeking to find out my entire life."

"We're thrilled you're seeking for answers, Kathy. It brings untold joys when we can bring more reality into our everyday lives. When we live our Light lives with our Light memories, there is a completely different process in our mind.

"Rising Light ways are gentle. No Light is harsh. This dedication to Light's skills must be joined in ourselves. This clarity of function of all things is seen as it really is. When our life touches inner life, we bring about a cooperation of our angelic food to always being used in our miracle ways.

"It seems like everyone thinks this fallen one is an angel. If one is an angel, this one does live all levels of itself in skilled internal action while moving its action in purity's Light in every level of itself. This is an angel completed. These are the angels that do go into the seeking-attaching skill of a person's mind an' assist with complete certainty of its task of giving Light that brings about change to a person's changing ways.

"Angels can only stay Light in their completion of birth. They cannot change out of what they have completed. The fallen one in history is not an angel. That's why this one fell. This one is not a completed angel. Completed angels are stabilized. They do penetrate any level, assist, adjust, an' transform themselves an' anyone else through sheer skill. But the person who changes themselves by the friendship of an angel will be wise to continue changing oneself an' continue the miracle ways of sustaining the level of angelic food given. These angels are our forever friends an' angelic family members that we enjoy so much from within us.

"As this fallen one is losing touch with an important part of itself, this one's world of Light does come apart. There is assistance for this person as this one declines. Angelic Light has skills of reviving inner Light leakage through a correct usage of Light.

"The journey to Hell travels out of this fall. Hell. What is Hell? Hell is the aftermath of a person almost birthed into a completed Light person, but this one's angelic food gets used out of the flow of protected life. So darkness blossoms through a process of us using the life of Light in ways it is never intended to be used.

"An' this is how this fallen one came to be such a known figure. This one is about to become a completed angel, an' misses a direction from self, an' changes into ways of being that have resulted in this one's reputation as we know of this fallen one today.

"Being as complete in Light ways an' then using all these Light ways in ways that carry no new Light, this person is missing out on using a skill in touching life with the action of going further into new parts of one's Light with using pure vision of seeing all things in ways they are put together,

"We are having benefits from angel people. They are bringing us our contacts out of our rising Light through themselves as they are assisting us into using our skill of changeable form. Our willingness as we're tapping our Light brings us home into the Light quickly.

"But you see, this fallen one changes direction in the middle of becoming birthed in Light ways. An' this is where the fall is happening. This is where the fallen one is missing these instructions in Heaven. This information of Heaven lives inside of us.

"This is where the fallen one is forming a Light body out of the beginnings of being in the forming womb of Light an' switches an' begins forming an unskilled Light body out of angelic Light, an' in these same moments begins turning self into unskilled ways of living. This one stops using Light in miracle ways right in the middle of being birthed into joyous ways.

"We only get one forever birth into Light. That's why this fallen one is being loved so much. We Light friends are doing all we can to reinforce this one to complete its form, a form that is used to live a life in our forever. Our birthing is in a constant active part of us.

"Our minds an' brains are made into Light swirls as we are birthing this activated Light way. When we are joined with our angelic brain action, we are safe an' properly functioning. There is only one function in the level of life we are at. This place we are in is to weave our Light body into a form that is in all ways functional.

"Nothing about the Earth level that is going on has anything to do with our reason for this level of life which is us having form in a miracle life. Our lives at this point are to weave ourselves into Light. As we are bringing our wholeness into a usabe brain an' outer part of us, we are blossoming a traveling self that has all the skills of angels. This is why some people say angels never live a life in darkness. This is true for some that always use themselves in the Light ways.

"But until one has blossomed its Light body, one's vulnerability is present. A misuse does bring a person into a weakening of one's outer body. An outer Light body uses attentiveness to its source.

"Our life's angelic food lives an' circulates as it is held in our inner protection. We know we are alive because of our angelic food. We begin our inner joys as we are blossoming into our forever life.

"So falling is a coming apart, an unraveling of one's life that once was blossoming oneself into an outer Light body. Without an outer part of us that belongs to the inner part of us, we will have no function in life. Without function in life we have nothing, no way to think or maneuver our self. Angelic Light is the sweetness that is our food that feeds us the inner Light way. With angelic Light food we thrive in miracle ways.

"So, the fallen one is nothing more than a Light person lacking its Light nutrition. People feel this person is an angel due to this one's misty formed Light self turning into skilled form that never did finish completing itself. People are confused about this fallen one. This rising Light in us is rejoined over an' over again an' begins this way of continuing the blossoming of the self into a formed Light person that does have all the misty formed Light ways in it for being able to continue itself into all of functional life. This is our automatic body ways of dancing in a joining with the living.

"We are in a perpetual motion of bringing a so-lidifying of ourselves through a superheterodyning miracle motion that is blossoming our body through ourselves. We are the fabric of our existence manifest-ing an' springing into ourselves an' attaching a miracle way of using our bodies that are the very heavens.

"Unskilled Light is a byproduct of not being an' making ourselves only into angelic Light. As we blos-som ourselves only into Light, we can see then that this is the only way for life to prosper is to keep ourselves only in miracle ways. Miracle ways bring automatic pro-tection an' brings us our understanding of our "viable volatile" substance that we are.

"This fallen one is still surrounded in purity's worlds that are living in depths of angelic swirls. This fallen one is not a bad character, an' neither are we when we tear up our outer body, our way, with our un-developed ability to use our life in Light.

"Yes, I hear you Kathy. I agree that any misuse of our attaching does bring unbelievable destruction, an' any skilled Light use of our attaching does bring unbelievable forever happiness. It's life-giving for us all to keep absorbing an' releasing a steady beat with us-ing ourselves in a way of blossoming our rising Light.

"The way life is being used by the fallen one, Kathy, is not the way of life. Life's' ways are joys. Life has a purpose, an' at this stage it's to complete a body for us to travel into Light worlds with. Our body is our stable point. Our body is our loop into Heaven's way of travel as we use twinkle air just like angels' breathe.

"There is no Hell. There is only the unraveling of oneself. As the fallen one is unraveling its life, this one no longer has a body that can sustain itself in heavenly ways. It's as simple as that, Kathy. Before angel we can be one such as this. We all have outer parts of us.

"An' at any moment we can find ourselves undoing our beautiful purity attachment that is making us this beautifully skilled traveling Light body an' life. So, the closer we get to being an angel, the more of us there is that can change into unskilled Light ways.

"The fall brings a long walk in the Light, as we go home, of putting oneself back together. The Humpty Dumpty rhyme has its place. It says we can't, but we can an' we are putting Humpty Dumpty back together again. Life does have its ways about it.

"We Light people are blossoming out of miracle run worlds. When one's Light food begins leaking out its life's angelic food, new ways of function swirl into form. Still well organized, but not at the rising functional levels, these people start decomposing an' all things so called "evil" are born. We still have life.

"Dropping is not life's way. Dropping is a journey undoing what has taken one so long to do. Whatever we do while we are not living in the rising angelic Lighted skills is useless to our lives. There is only value in the ways of life in miracles. Our formed part of us has one purpose. This is to give us function in Light. I am saying that life is simpler than we may think, Kathy.

"The cold an' hot dark pits of Hell is the weakened parts of the skilled Light body of a fallen one's life, for the skilled Light body no longer has the skilled Light nourishment of the full amount of angelic food fed to it.

As one is starving from no Light, this one declines. This one's Light body becomes lifeless an' does not activate its Light areas due to lack of angelic water moistening its seeds. This one is once almost joined an' set in place by this angelic birthing of its Light form.

"This person sadly comes apart an' leaves a way of life that becomes very painful for itself an' angels that chose to get involved. This fallen one is beginning an active blossoming of a body out of Light from remnants of what is left of this one's angelic seeds, an' is again using its attaching skills in Light ways to bring this one home into finished Light in form.

"If we use Light an' fumble an' fall, we must continue reaching for Light nutrition from self. Some of us fumble an' fall from much more Light ways in us. Kindness an' love is what's needed for all of us. The closer one is to being a completed Light person, if they fall, the more of no Light ways they bring into their form, the more love they can use.

"Remember, we like love an' friendship from angels as much as fallen Light people like love an' friendship from us. The fallen one can use love an' still does. The fallen one is a person like we are, an' is trying to become an angel just as we are trying to become an angel which is nothing more than completing our outer Light vehicle of our self. We are a while in the making as we are blossoming angelic traveling wings.

"We are in a purpose of remembering levels of our fun life in an internal Lighted attaching to our twinkling depths. So nice enjoying our Lighted forevers inside of us. It's so nice to know the value of making a self for the real purpose of a person's life lived at all levels of itself with a fun, sparkly body made out of its own abilities so this person can function an' have everything met by its own skill. We are awakening our beauty an' seeing the way it truly is in the sparkle ways, an' we are finding all within us bubbling up through us with fresh new ideas. An' we are seeing it all an' living it all in life as we turn our gaze into the wellspring of our own self's love for us. Our own love is the most loving love ever.

"The Light in us knows how to live this life that we are, an' our Light does tell us the ways of skilled Light an' unskilled Light. Ask an' listen to our life within us. Life is open to all of us. We all have the faculties to hear an' understand the truth of ourselves in the livingness process that we are involved in. Life is our guide, our mentor. Life is a living attachment to us that lives in us an' is us. There are lots of ways Light touches us an' brings us inward, an' upward, downward, an' sideways into life's many places of Light.

"Heaven becomes a friend as we live more an' more the heavenly ways. Heaven comes out of the way we live our life. We are blossoming ourselves, an' we are blossoming ourselves into worlds of Light.

"We, in our automatic loving ways of action, put sweet Light into every aspect of us having an' allowing life to wield all of our life's worlds with us. Life is ours.

"An' this fun nectar that is the person's Light food is the difference between a person falling out of heavenly ways or a person staying in heavenly ways."

This information has stopped coming into me, an' I am relaxing in this lovely place. My angel is returning to greet me with her loving smile an' glittering Light flowing out of her fingertips. This sweet Light person is escorting me into an isolated room an' is saying if I like I can speak to this fallen one directly since I have no fear an' understand the ways that this one's life is taking. I am gladdened with happiness. My angel is saying this one is looking forward to my visit. It will be a short moment being with this person, but nevertheless a moment to remember for sure. I understand the goodness in our meeting.

The fallen one is coming into this room with several large angels surrounding this one. This person is looking at me with love an' tears dripping down this lovely face. This person looks a lot like the moment in the lovefest. I inwardly hear this fallen one's knowings an' understandings from deep down in a place within this one for the discomfort I personally am going through in these ages of this one's coming apart.

It's precious what I'm feeling. This fallen one is recognizing me far into Light's history, remembering my life's joining that I am living in while this one's lifeline is leaking beautiful Light into worse than nowhere.

This one can bring some of itself into Light now. What a pleasant change. It is this one's usage of attaching angels' Light that is making the changes happen. There are extreme, intense exchanges in this one as angel Light is finding its way of layering rising Light's food as its reviving substance. This all is bringing strength back so this person can activate Light usage in its travels into deeper Light. It's necessary to be self-directed while activation takes place.

This person is hugging me with love an' Light at a distance. This love is beautiful. I am being made aware by the angels that this one's joy of me an' my daunting stamina in this person's behalf has been an integral part in this one's travels in returning to Light.

This fallen person is graciously leaving the room, an' I am better for the sharing for I love, an' have always loved, all of life's children. Even as a little girl, I often in my mind spoke kindness to this fallen one an' said, "go to Jesus, an' Jesus will be there to be your friend an' do whatever is necessary."

I find myself in a miracle way appearing on my little unicorn, flying full speed through scenery that is as beautiful as the sun's sparkles on the ocean. I'm free in Light, an' so is the fallen one. This sparkle road home has more than begun. This one is sure y going through the wringer from its life while using life in unhappy ways. I am becoming aware of my body on Earth, so I am leaving the Light ways of seeing things.

THE SPLASH: I hear this in my mind. "The splash, Kathy, this splash effect I am telling you about, sweet child, is our angels' way of living. It's like the ocean waves splashing up against the rocks, sending droplets of water flying everywhere Kathy. So in our moments, we act an' live the splashing moments.

"We want to share with you, Kathy, splashing is where our life is. So always we are up, in a way, where life is new an' ever moving in the miracle of the splash an' not the fixed mind thinking that brings the grueling issue to life. But we are Kathy up into what brings the grueling issue into the splash of resolution. Everything about us comes from within us. Spark your resolve."

The joy these people-angels bring into me I love so much.

20
Rising Light (Part 3)

My unicorn an' I are sitting under a tree with pink blossoms on it, awaiting answers. In the meantime, we are enjoying the butterflies. We have decided to take a dip into the dancing ponds of fun, sparkling, liquid Light.

Nature sprites are taking a dip with us. They are just appearing in the air an' are adorned in crystalline, twinkly colors. I love them so much. My angels are appearing out of sparkles, an' are smiling with a joy of happiness. This sharing is beginning.

I have a question about something that is said about the fallen one in my last writing. "As you know, Yellow Rose Angel, we only know of the ways of Light when the fallen Light one is in the glowing love an' entering an' blossoming into an angel level. This is long ago, in this far distant Light world where we all are blossoming perfectly an' lovingly in our own ways.

"Twirling an' enjoying our tumbling an' evolving in the Light as all Light babies an' Light people do, life is grand an' all harmonious with purity ways in all of us. Even this fallen person. We are born in Light, an' still living in Light.

"So, Yellow Rose Angel, all is well with life an' people. There is no suffering an' no pain. So, this has left me a little perplexed. The pain an' suffering came because of the fallen one's fall an' after the fallen one's fall. So, Yellow Rose Angel, would you please enlighten me on all this? I would so like to hear."

"It is the simple fact, Kathy, that this fallen person is becoming a most beautiful Light person an' is becoming ever so thrilled as we all do as we are birthed out of our misty Light's beautiful ways.

"The joy of it all, it's like something that is the best joys ever. These life's purities an' exquisite forms that are happening to this one just innocently overtakes this Light angelic person. Life is becoming so wonderful that this one just cannot stop admiring the blossoming of self being formed into Light worlds an' spectacular ways. This precious Light person is in the grips of being fully birthed into angelic worlds to live in.

"This one is enjoying this process so much in this perfected beauty that this one begins hovering too long. This hovering, looking, an' enjoying is what releases this one's Light food. This begins a different blossoming with life's ways for this one. So, with the enjoyment, this one's birthing process is stopping an' is taking itself out of its natural Lights birthing.

"It leaves the Lighted ways that it is headed into. This life of this person is in a most angelic movement, a dynamic flow. It is blossoming up its purest self for more changeable action that is bringing it into other places in its inner Light ways. So just by this one hovering, it instantly begins stopping the high-rising Light that is taking this one into full angelic skilled form. Automatically this one begins a new usage of self, not in the rising Light of self, but at the unskilled Light of self.

"An' this is why this fallen one is a so talked about person. This one's internal action begins changing direction in itself, not meaning to stop its angel completion but this one has no choice since angelic nutrition is our blossoming fuel.

"Kathy, life is simpler than we know. This fallen one's beauty in being in its original life an' enjoying it in a freewheeling, unguarded way leaks Light food. We must keep our placement of ourselves contained an' blossoming as we are being our skills in action. It's just that the beauty of ourselves is spectacular to behold, as the fallen one is seeing.

"We must accept our profound beauty as a natural way of ourselves an' keep our aliveness pure that we wield in our everyday life, an' give it the gentle acknowledgement it deserves. When we notice our beauty, it is to be a natural blossoming within us, no special attention put on it. Just know that we are being life's magnificence.

"This one begins noticing an' enjoying this beautiful form, this spectacular, colorful blossoming of itself. This is such a wonderful, joyous time for us in life. This is all okay if the releasement of our life's joined forces is guiding the action. Then complete protection will be there in rising Light."

"Sad to me, sweet Yellow Rose Angel."

"Yes Kathy, it is. This Lighted one just hovered too long in recognition of bringing into itself these moments of becoming more of the skills that kind life has for us. This is the first time this one is beginning to become formed in a way of solidifying skilled Light into an outer, tangible, functional, connected, layered, visible, personalized formed self that does only know the first misty forming of our heavenly start in life's womb.

"You see Kathy, as we are coming out of our beginnings of misty ways of living, we enter an' awaken our visible Light part of our birthing. A part of us that attaches. Attaching that understands its life an' death ways is what brings our completed Light body into form. An' being personalized brings us into seeing ourselves an' others from the outside in. An' now seeing our angelic form from the outside of us brings a new skill for me an' you to use in our Light usage of our self.

"An' this is where the fallen one is solidifying its stable form. This new way is so very exciting to this one, being in the middle of its birthing an' all. This is where this one begins hovering too long enjoying the stunning life it is. This visual excitement process draws too much angelic food out of this one an' leaves it with less of its lifeforce. Now there is not enough angelic food to complete its Light body.

"These are very crucial moments. This is a natural outcome when attaching blossoms differently. An' at this point, this one's life function begins anew automatically. This change is bringing a turning of events for this person, so now new actions an' guidance is releasing from within this person an' it takes charge instantly in a way of undoing its joined, natural birthing.

"Life's Light ways cannot keep the inner life together an' going into angel-changing action without the person's full attachment an' direct personal angelic food releasing into a joining in this transformation. But now because this one begins an automatic becoming anew through this process of excitement, this one's angelic food is no longer pure life but depleted life an' unable to nourish the Light directions.

"So, no longer is rising Light continuing its blossoming of these worlds of living Light for this one. The moment uses all attachment an' all life's processes from self, an' sometimes a sparkle of angels' Light, to complete one's outer Light body. This hovering an' enjoying, as innocent as it is, nevertheless, life lives in a particular way.

"An' this one loses contact with the rising Light of self that is bringing this one into purity ways. This one's forming an' using Light skills is necessary to be able to sustain itself in the next action of living in the next rung of one's many Light worlds that they are a part of.

"This one cannot quickly turn around life's moving life that is used for the rising Light to be present enough to make the blossoming happen for this one in this moment.

"The outcome is this fallen one becomes a person without enough joined Light in the body to feed itself the living water of life that is necessary for a miracle life to continue. The life's angelic food is our navigator. No longer is there enough angelic food to navigate this one into miracle living.

"Angelic food is an attached part of us, a thinking part of us, a seeing part of us, an' a hearing part of us. With plenty of angelic food, our life functions. The ecosystem of our misty forming of our entire self over eons is perfectly blossoming for us a personalized entire heavenly life an' is bringing a looping of our jeweled, forever, beautiful, fun, happy angel body into a finished birth. This is the place that never happened for this fallen one. Not yet anyway. But it will, an' is, happening as life continues its birthing process for this one.

"This is a little explanation, Kathy. Life is an automatic function. Our life is to be lived intrinsically within ourselves as a joining with forever ways in sweet miracles. We are a skillful life's action that brings life alive, a forever joining with the forever in happiness.

"Movement with life is our life an' is the balance that is within each person's joyous Light ways. Without life's angelic food being in motion an' balance, all life will turn into less potent Light. Then there will be very little life movement to keep things fresh an' viable.

"Without movement an' one's retained viable angelic food that is generated by self an' now with angels' input, life cannot be vibrant at any level. Our joys blossom ourselves out of deeper Light levels an' continuous ways of being sunny Light.

"The only way we can continue life is by using our own personal self in an internal progression of pulsing each speck of our lives with using our own nectar made by our very own inner selves. It's a personal skill we develop with our nectar that lives inside of us. This in us becomes the stairway to Heaven, an' only can Heaven be reached in just this way, Kathy, an' this way only Kathy. The fallen one did not go to the next level in the way, an' only way it can be done.

This one's fall is not life's doing. Life did not kick the fallen one out of life's heavens. This one's lifeline is leaking out its Light's food which brings an unhealthy, pleasurable feeling to it. An' in this happening, life's Light function cannot continue in the same sweet ways.

"An' in this, this person falls an' naturally begins losing its life's cohesive ways of using itself. So this one becomes a different level, an' begins functioning in the Light unskilled place within itself springing up the garden of Eden's lifestyle. This is life's way—always changing. This person in these many moments since life became formed the way it did for this one is now being able to regain some of the rising Light action through selected careful usage of this one's personally made alive nectar action within itself.

"This one is being able to do this with the continuous assistance of the angels. An' this fallen one is now understanding the volatile function an' usages of one's lifeforce, an' is also seeing the process of life's angelic food bringing congealment into an external life. We love this fallen one. Can you see why, Kathy?"

"This person is one of us."

"Yes Kathy, this is true. We love all of life".

As she says this, our joys touch an' colorful sparkles begin twinkling between us. So sweet.

"Things are ever changing, Kathy. On a subtle level, all life is moving. It has a sparkling quality to it that is life's pulse. It is in stable, refined movements in the inner places of ourselves. Life has it all figured out, Kathy. One uses the self to continue the self. We each only have oneself to use, an' that's our own.

"There will always be a level of an outer body that we are. The level of the outer body continues to become more capable in Light skills an' beauty. Eventually, outer parts of people will sparkle an' change out of the depleted Light ways. This fall is not our life. It is a miserable mess for this person an' all concerned. The continuous nows of this one's fall is lived in a protected bubble kept away from the worlds an' the ways of the living angels an' their homes.

"This disaster has kept us from the real ways of living our lives. We are assisting all people to grab ahold of oneself an' keep its own angelic food protected, an' always to understand the valuable substance that lives inside of us.

"All life that gets caught up in this fall becomes exiled with this fallen one. Including an angel. No one can get out, an' no one can get in. It's a hell worse than any hell. An' this is the time of the angel-created bubble being popped. An innocent mistake still has the extreme battles to get back to purity's usage of one's self, an' one still has to live in the ways of misuse until one can start blossoming healthy usage.

"An' all life that is in this bubble of miracle love is being released back into life's loving ways. The fall is to be forgotten. Nothing gained, much destroyed. Gain can only be had when one functions in life's miracle ways which is what the fallen one is doing now. We're getting out of unspeakable ways of living.

"The fallen one is climbing out of these misuses an' overuses of its lifeline. There is a lot of unhappy to be reversed. It took eons to get this one into being malnourished to the degree that this fallen one is thinking life an' the angels do not love this one an' do not care about this fallen one anymore, when in fact the love to Heaven is always open for reentry. The entrance is within each of our ways of using ourselves. Enter an' swirl into the colors within our Heaven by using our attaching skills as we're flowing our living us.

We do use our Light's angelic food to blossom us as we live in an attached Light way.

"You're free to traverse all miracle worlds. Pools of Light are springing up in us. Remember your birthing out of Light, Kathy. An' remember your unskilled Light body is valuable to you, Kathy. It is still you. It's your tool of spinning life. With it, you have life forever. Without it, you have no tool for yourself to use.

"Your body will pulse an' become a skilled beauty. But remember the uses for an outer an' inner body will always be. A bubble has been created out of life's reviving skills. This bubble is individually an' collectively feeding transformational insights into each person's life. An' each person's now freedoms hinges on this absorption of their life's activity with life directly. Life loves us, an' all we have to do is to love it back an' to allow ourselves to be the life that is connected love.

"We spring our own angelic food of life's beauty into our angelic self. The long disconnect we have been under to protect the angels' homes, this was necessary, for the safety of life's levels are easily damaged from the fallen one's lack of its life's angelic food being used in miracle ways. Inner mind traveling brings you your life. It is so different being the you you really are. Light minds are fragile so we use extreme care.

"Kathy, I would like to say to you an' your sweet sparkle friends reading that when free will in Light ways are finished being developed at angels' level, then angels are ready to use their skill of free will to assist people if they choose to. There is no free will till angel development is completed. Free will is the angel purity of a body completion of being birthed in rising Light."

21
Rising Light (Part 4)

I am going within my Love Garden within my mind while my earthly part of me sits quietly awaiting with pen an' paper to write down the answers to my question I have for my yellow rose angel.

My Light self loves to travel inwardly into these pretty worlds of glistening love an' sparkling gardens. With my feet in the soothing river waters, my lovely yellow rose angel appears. She sits down beside me.

"Kathy, you are wanting to know about this golden look of the fallen person going into this angels' love ceremony. Well, I will tell you a little about how life's beauty is working through Jesus.

"Alive gold is the center of our body of Light that is our life living an' providing in spirit. Jesus has been sharing this personal gold part of self with the fallen one in a joining to hold this one together with strands of gold Light that is coming out of Jesus' life an' soul.

"Our life's angelic gold is our forever us. That's why gold cannot be used up. It's our forever soul. So, the same us we use in miracle ways is the same us we use as we are declining. The miracle food is what brings us life either way. If our Light food is used through forming it not into rising Light ways, it weakens us. It still releases our life's skills to bring us all things we use by us, but through a different type of exchange. So, we begin surviving in another way. They both are us living our lives in whatever way we are living it. We people are the food creator that is making us.

"Jesus' angelic, sparkling, golden oscillation does bring this fallen one angelic food. This is because this fallen one's Light food is drained out so thoroughly that Jesus an' angels use their food's lifeline in harmony with this one's depleted food's lifeline to spring this one's self into miracle activities with itself.

"It takes a lot of Lighted food from a person or persons that use their Light food in miracle ways to assist another person back into purity usage of themselves. It's a way of feeding Light's food into one.

"When we use life in changing our Light's activities from a flow of angelic miracles into an action that is separating us from the dynamic flow of the ways of living miracles, we then begin leaking our sparkling food into a solid. That's where physical food, gold coins, animals, an' all condensed, separated life come from. It is created out of our entire soul's creation of itself.

"All this solid gold, an' all things of this one's denseness, will have to be Light sparked out of its heaviness to get back into its swirling Light that is forming us. We people are letting Jesus into ourselves as we are thinking of Jesus. We begin remembering our sparkling golden soul is our provider twinkling our life's everything in our personalized Light body.

"A joining in this one Jesus brings people into being able to be using their own miracle self in a direct way. This contact with Jesus is us being returned into attaching to life. We begin being revived by Jesus' willingness to share this living golden lifeline with us. Jesus is releasing life's food's goodness into us while streaming Jesus' living ways into us. This is bringing our memories back to us of our miracle beginnings, an' coddling us back into our natural function. An' this is why the fallen one is on the upswing of life lived now.

"This is Jesus' process an' beauty. Jesus is giving us this shared lifeline that is still living in alive heavenly ways to revive us an' bring us home to real ways where all life joins with life that keeps our Light life surviving. This all is happening only when life is left to run our lives in miracle ways only. Jesus an' angels are our safety net for us children that have trouble being the living, Lighted, attaching ways of life. We are in a survival mode instilling within ourselves skills to spring ourselves back into being only alive.

"Now that we are birthing our outer body through the way of attaching through joy an' happiness, our living journey in beautiful Light ways of living in the womb of Light are now joining us as we are becoming now our Light body. Yet unbeknownst to us, we've been making ourselves into a dying Light person.

"Some of us never does detach from the living way. We become vibrant Light sparkles. We become a beautiful form living an' enjoying as we are continuing our playing together in Light as we do in our beginnings of us being droplets of water an' sunlight glistening us into each other's company in areas of our inner love contacts with each other.

"Being aware of being fed on Light's angelic food an' drinking from our droplets of water that are joined inside of us, it's our own inner sun Light nour-ishment with life's natural ways of eating from within side our Light centers in us. This is in keeping with be-ing cared for by the miracle ways that we all will again only live an' breathe from a place of making an' using all things inside of us. Our truest savior is in our self.

"We are drawing into us tiny sparks out of silver, shiny ponds—receiving life's assistance into an' attach-ing this alive way of becoming whole. Our completion of us living our lives out of life's ways of keeping us alive an' happy from being in a flow with a life only liv-ing—is us relying on life to know best in a world alive.

"That's all it is, Kathy. We are the fireflies shim-mering like perfected rhinestones, multicolored prisms shining forth as we fly around this paradise, always changing an' being life lived. It's you an' me dancing in life from no form into misty form that blossoms into our vibrant, personalized, stable, skilled Light form.

"We are life lived an' lived an' lived in different forms with different capabilities right into the form of angel, glowing, coming an' going at will, developed an' skilled in living all living things to now being extraordi-narily happy an' adept at skilled movement.

"This is the way it is in our womb in Light before our seed of attaching becomes activated an' after our blossomed attaching births us into functional Light people. Life brings clarity an' shines on us a necessity of existing with an outer part of us such as a contained Light body that we can use with our forever lives.

"A person's personalized Light substance used in heavenly ways is dynamic an' flowing in very quick, speedy ways of pulsing through right away, sparkling into any place we want to go like in the way's angels an' more developed people do. But when one's vibrant Light ways are leaking Light food, then one has to maneuver oneself in their outer forms of themselves that are weakening. No longer is one turning self into a Lighted person, but starving oneself into a separation from many ways of oneself. These ways then become an' are one's surviving ways. So money, food, an' lots of stuff like everything about us is an unhinged usage of the ways of life that once functioned in the natural, joined self in Light's internally active, vibrant ways is no longer the way of life for this fallen one.

"Since this one does not weave its lifeline through sustained Lighted attaching back into its lifeline an' keep this constant attaching in this blossoming of itself into Light, then one must now live an' survive in any way they can. So as they turn themselves into no new Light, what was has now changed for them.

"Life's safety net is in all of us. In Light ways of living, one sparkles in ease an' grace. Without the joining with oneself in miracle ways, one gasps for breath.

"Miracle ways are weaving us a Light body into a form an' is doing this through us being attached to it. Having a Light form brings one's contacts into every Light level one is an' every Light level one is becoming.

"One's nectar used not in Light ways then will become anew in a debilitating way. This also is an actual, natural effect. If one no longer is blossoming Light into Light for one's forever to continue in Light, then life automatically then begins to form one into the ways we are living now. So that's what is called the fall of man. What it really is is the fall of one's usage of self.

"Kathy, you want to know why the ways of us on the deepest, darkest ways about us brings such strict effects on the most insidious, inhumane realities that people are enduring. The reason things are the way they are is us people. We're centered into the middle of our silver pond, drawing into us sparkles of traveling Light. As these shiny pinpoints of gently attaching twinkles keep arriving, an' we continue allowing these shooting threads of Light to bring us new Light levels of skills, then our lives will stay in stable balance.

"There is no group of people that brings dark ways upon another. It's the person themselves that bring the dark ways through the way they use their life. We people are in a survival mode in whatever undeveloped dark action we find ourselves involved in.

"Kathy, to act an' do all the things people do to people in dark ways is because Light brings directions that are not being picked up an' used by us.

"These ways we have become, it's all we have an' know to do an' be at this place we find ourselves in now. It's natural for us to function in the ways our inner part of us releases out of our internal history.

"We must insist that we use Light blossoming of our Light seeds only so that only Light seeds will blossom us, no more dark seed blossoming will take place. Then we are free from being entangled in the web of creation gone wrong. It's our inner seeds bringing us our residence. I must be on my Light way, Kathy."

22

Loving One's Self

Angels have so many skilled ways to intervene in us.

I am suffocating. The moment is still alive in me.

My 1st father is enjoying his two daughters so much that he brings them both into being with child. I became with child first. I would not have me removed from me. The child in my womb is me. So, my first father put a pillow over my face an' suffocated me an' our unborn baby. This reality lives in me.

I love me an' coddle me as I comfort me through these moments in knowings. I am aware as life's ways surface in me. Love an' much care I must give myself to bring me to a place of peace. These things within me come up in me to be listened to.

My 2nd father is my first father, an' my sister at that time becomes my new mother. An' this is when I become removed from my protected place. I am yelling out from my very being, "Don't take my body. Please, don't take my body," as the person is removing me from my new mother's womb.

I'm hovering above the table, so afraid. The space is lifeless. No human connection to make contact to anything. I am in a clear bubble, pushing with my little fingers, trying to get out, break through, breathe, but I can't pop my partly developed fingers through this clear film. I am feeling unbelievable feelings. A hell. Very eerie. Barren. Shaken to my core.

I am seeing the person doing the removal of me an' my body. I am watching it an' having it done to me all at the same time. My being is screaming as my outer contact with this world is being severed in such a ghastly way.

I don't have anywhere to go. My home is being removed from me an' my safe haven where I am tucked away comfortably within my new mother's womb. An' all of this is ending. An' not only ending, but is ripping an' tearing, frying my brain with pain an' terror. This is all so, so very difficult to get through.

My recovery in this is wrenching. So the far-reaching effects into myself are truly here. My love knows how to give to me an' understands my horror. I am allowing myself to bring into me this that is me.

I am absorbing me into my heavenly Light, an' loving me, an' giving me Light colors I need for my beauty into my forever life. Life's love is great, an' we are the fixers of our own selves.

An' as I am bringing this up in me, feeling an' re-experiencing an' remembering, this is the process for me fixing me. My life's living moments are being revived. Us caring for ourselves is necessary for our life to be coddled an' loved by us, in us, an' through us. Each one of us does this for ourselves. It will always be this way, an' it always has been this way.

My 3rd father is physically enjoying me for his pleasures in my first two an' a half years of my little life. I am his play toy. But for me, the lifeforce drain hurts me. It is painful to be in an exchange of lifeforce with a person much more developed than mine, me being a newborn baby an' all. My new daddy's penetration on me with his intent on me to stimulate his pleasure zones draws too much of my life out of me an' leaves me depleted, drained, hurting in ways that leaves me suffering so much that I have to leave again through death. So, my 3rd try for a flesh life failed.

For my 4th try at getting a father there is a new change my angels are doing with me. I am becoming aware of myself on a white cloud sitting with my legs dangling over the edge, with angels talking to me. The angels this time want me not to enter through the womb again since the last three times ended so drastically. An' so, they're showing me a life I can have.

There is a little girl that wants out of her life due to her stepgrandfather is taking liberties with her. The angels told me that I would be someone that the girl's father would get along with an' that after I enter the body that is 2½ years of age then my new father will come an' get me from Grandpa's an' Grandma's house, where the little girl lives, an' I will be safely removed an' go to live with the mom an' dad.

The angels are showing me the first part of my life I will have, an' it seems quite hard an' I do not want to go. Now they're showing me the second part of my life, an' it is wonderful. So, as I am feeling the wonderful, these angels are placing me in this body I am in now. I am awakening on a hand-carved antique couch. The pillow smells real nice. I'm looking around an' getting up off the couch. I have a pretty little dress on. My fourth try is a success. People call me "Kathy."

I hold my love nice an' close; an' I wrap it tightly around me. An' even though I may not see or feel my love, it is in every way still here with me.

A joyous night: I am sitting outside under the stars. Crying. An angel appears an' holds me close with her angel arms all aglow with kind love as I'm releasing painful moments through tears.

One day a hummingbird is watching me while I'm sleeping off an' on in bed for two days. This hummingbird, several times each day, comes to my window, sits on the same branch, in the very same place on the branch every time she comes back. I do look at her till I go to sleep each time. As I'm waking up, she is coming back each time. The end of the second day I am feeling better. She leaves, comes back with her teeny tiny babies. She wants me to see her family. Her love to me is her feeding me her life.

Our birth is precious. I would like to ask all life if it could: Could you hold me like an angel? Could you love me like a charm? Would you keep me close an' tender in your loving arms, to hold me like an angel, to live with hope an' charm as we dance this life together in the sunshine of eternal life? Could you hold me like an angel? Could we sing our songs of life as we live in worlds of angels through the skies at night? Loving every moment, we are together in the pitch of eternal life. So, keep loving me like an angel an' treating me like a charm, bringing hope to each other in the sunshine of our inner life. Could you love me like an angel? Could you hold me like a charm? Could you love me? Could you hold me? Could you keep me close in the Light?

23
Life's in Our Hands

I'm pouring my Light through my fingers as they're touching my hair as I'm joining my sleep. The Light in my hair sparks with the depths of my life's travel, so I glisten with my heavenly life through my hands. My ears dance in delight as a protective feeling soothes me so much. My mouth gets so happy to feel these soothing rays as my eyes smile for joy as they await their turn from my palm's rays. As we use our Light, we gain our life. Our hands are helping us use Heaven.

We can only bring our Light body into being with plenty of Light nutrition. This nectar that we are is making our inner an' outer lives survive in harmony as heavenly ways become our normal.

We are lifeforce for the day's living. Be aware of our palms of our hands sparkling Light, an' let our miracles happen in us. Let the softness of our skills move our Light by gently putting our palms over us an' resting our hands on ourself. This then is feeding us nutrients.

Our hands bring soothing showers in soft Light towards us. Also, as we twirl one way an' then twirl the other way we become more vibrant. Twirl quickly or slowly. As we tickle our skin lightly with our nails, we'll have more active life as we give ourselves attention.

This extra aliveness brings us much more into love's Light. It's a joyous way to live. Getting up off the floor an' grass, this sparkles really well for sharing circlets of Light. So, all of this extra action in us is quite a gentle way to bring our Light springs alive.

This Light that we are is very friendly. I use me to rev me up by letting the living miracle nectar pour through the palms of my hands into the bottom of my feet. So beautiful, being giving to myself. Inner sunlight swirling out of our hands, moving over our skin, brings us joy by releasing, attaching, an' closing the living angelic circlets as they come out of us into us.

This all brings about a stream of sparkling motions through our palms. This brings our life's colors into balance into our Light layers of our self. We receive swirls of Light streams, an' the Light of us is bringing us our inner life from the outside in. Squeezing my skin gently releases air, then I feel better.

The outer part of us brings strength to hold onto us, our invisible self that is not really invisible. We can give to this outer us by getting some wonderful, instant pick-me-ups by allowing the palms of our hands to release this alive nectar directly into us from us. This will keep the pinpoints of Light within our body strong. We must be able to hold us, our living self of stupendous Light. We have a fun body. It is our Heaven's doorway.

As we're housing a self, such as us, the structure is to be made out of our purest selves. We are impenetrable diamond pinpoints of starlight shields having the ability to shield out an' hold in.

This is what our visible parts of ourselves purpose is. It's a shield we bring into form for the purpose of a functional place that we carry as our life source. This is our creator within us forever. We have special freedoms. We can go wherever we want to be. Maneuvering our self is the reason for a body of skilled Light. We have skills, so we will go like an angel is known to go taking their entire self with them. In a flash they appear, an' in a flash they disappear. In a twinkle of a sparkle they are here, an' then they're not.

This is what I am talking about. Us skilled in maneuvering ourselves in ways Light people do. What a wonderful way to live. Like all living things, outer parts of us are usable to the actions of the inhabitant. Our outer parts are our inner self becoming. The strength of us depends on the way of our usage of rising Light.

The insides of us an' the outsides of us are to be sparked out of shields of sparkles that are protected from any action other than our duty to ourselves. The strength of duty depends on us. As we are of angelic Light thinking, then this usage of life's ways will bring strength to us. This brings us into being a Light person.

The wonderful worlds of Light are what we are becoming as we're blossoming from within. We must do many things due to the fact that we are the artists of such a way. We blossom us out of our own life. We use our very self as the angelic glow thread of Light that we weave into our miracle that is us. We are the genie in a bottle. We are the goose that lays the golden egg.

Our bodies are the determining factor whether we are crying, the sky is falling, the wolf blew our house down, or someone stole our golden egg. All of these fairytale stories are referring to a very real happening in our lives. When one is tearing down or builds up the outer part of themselves, this is the determining factor of our existence. Our life takes hold here.

We can assist this part of ourselves. The living us is totally in control of us. We are misty love finding ourselves becoming form as we go along. The whole purpose of ourselves is to live an' to always renew our outer protection for our inner use. It is a necessary part of us. Only with form can we survive in our forever.

Even angelic people have form in skilled layers made out of their life into an outer receiver for themselves. That's what we see when we see an angelic person. Their outer appearance looks like pastel diamonds. Every living thing has an outer visible part.

A person is made into condensed lifeforce, the life of our self. Us. We are the stuff that becomes everything as we know it. We are the very life of us. We are the living life all around us. From the very fibers of our own life, all life is formed. It is the same for angels.

We can change the structure of Light because we are Light. An' we do reuse Light, as we must do because we update our thinking due to us living into worlds of our forever. An' our outer us blossoms always. Life is something we will always be in. It's something we go into. We must take the glow thread of Light to guide us into deeper Light layers of ourselves.

If we have seen a Light person, we have seen their outer part of them is pure an' gentle, solid, an' filled with thick rainbow layers an' prisms shining out many streamers of sweet beauty. These angels have awakened into a lovely, functioning them.

Having such a home an' vehicle in themselves took these one's life lived in a happy way of listening to one's love within oneself, an' following one's inner guidance, an' enjoying one's own company. What a delight to know that this is also in me, that I too am something as spectacular as this. An' to think that all people are such is wonderful to me. The wonders of life always are when one blossoms Light.

I am glad we are all in this life thing forever. This is a nice gift that always gives. Let's give the gift of Light to each other. An' let's make sure that we give to life, just as the sun gives its sustenance of life so life can live this miracle we are.

Yes, our bones are active an' making Light as we're bringing us into miracle ways. My brain is my mind that is forming me into what I am using for me to be able to express myself. Our body is activating our soul's gold-diamond-jeweled core. Our souls are us.

We can turn our palms of our hands toward our body, an' the rays will travel into our skin even without touching the skin. We do also release streamers as our attached jeweled mind brings circlets out of an' into us through a colorful array of skilled Light that is changing our unskilled body, mind, brain, an' thinking into becoming a usable form that we can enjoy forever.

Light sparkles are in abundance as we squeeze our entire body from the inside out all in the same moment. Releasing an' gently squeezing again an' again in us speeds up a swirling around us of colors spinning in many directions. This sparks every level of our life. It's fun an' brings us attachments into our Light food.

So nice for me sharing an' being a part of your sparkle in this moment. We do touch each other, even at great distances, because love travels.

24

Sweetness Opens Light

I'm entering through a Light swirl in myself, an' am sitting by a lake, listening to singing water trickling through fields of flowers, when an angelic girl appears an' begins speaking to me about how-to bring people into happy thinking. I am writing down what she is saying. Other people in Light are gathering an' listening in.

This angelic girl touches everyone in love colors. These precious visiting people are sharing back littler circlets of love to the angelic girl. I can feel the excitement as it builds with each arrival. This interaction has lit up the garden area with a glow of love colors.

Our angelic girl is saying, "We can catch any thinking in unskilled Light or skilled Light an' shine into it with our love, an' the sweetness that is in this love is blossoming our structure of our thinking. We can shine ourselves into any part of us an' bring changes in our self in any way we choose. Thinking is a boat of travel.

"Our thinking in love is our nectar's movement abundantly flowing into us in a constant way, fully releasing in an automatic feeding into our thinking. When one's lifeline is leaking love, this is where the twist into pain an' suffering enters into our lives. We are now in a scramble to rearrange our thinking that is leaking out our angelic nutrients. This is how life has changed out of our healthy, natural abundance of our perfect birth."

"This is so sad, angel girl. Thank you for telling us." She smiles with so much shine in her beautiful self.

"So until your leakage of Light is restored, this is what to do to savor every drop of nectar we receive. Think of anything in life that is going on within you, then look in on it with love-Light an' you will see it dissolve away in the way it is being seen by you, an' you will now be experiencing it in a new, fresh you.

"This way of becoming you will determine you an' other people as it can also delight you because it puts you in a new way with yourself.

"So where did all the other ways of looking at you go? They vanish with a click of a sweetness attachment. All is different in love life, as it always is an' always has been. It's us that lives each moment of our life in the confines of our own self.

"Sweetness created beauty, abundance, an' happiness. It's all ours for the taking. Reach inward. Your Light springs are overflowing. Use your diamond-golden gearshift an' Heaven's jeweled kaleidoscopic compass to think you lovingly into your angel self.

"Any being that functions in love, functions in sweetness. It's a twist of the attaching thinking that makes it one thing or another. We are the ones that make our own mental views in life an' become the mental views in our own self. This is where our life counts. Moment to moment, we are the only ones in us.

"We make the moves. See in sweetness everything so your life will be sweetness. If we really want to be honest with ourselves, we will function in the truth that all things are put together through a process of internal usage of our self. Whatever our life's usages may become, it always is us living life from our own devices. If you are thinking into something an' decide that's not what you want it to be, just change your attaching into a willingness of allowing a sweetness way of thinking into it an' you will change it.

"You have all you will ever have in you now for internal life lived in the most feeling good, freeing instructions of a joyous way to be. You have everything within you that internal angelic ones have to perfect their selves in forever Light living. Continue your thinking in the thinking of angelic ones. It is natural for us because we are one of them. A child of the Light."

My life is beginning to return to earthly ways now. The angelic girl an' others are all returning to where they came from, just as I am now becoming aware, more an' more, of me on Earth. The miracle entrance into Light has closed an' I am better for the adventure into my fun self an' angel ways of living.

As all of these angel's messages rise up in pure, loving Light, we get to feel things from them that we have never before felt. Angels an' Light people release messages from their orbs of Light into our orbs. They have the love to shine us into our caring for ourselves an' holding us there awhile so we can feel the reasons for our angelic food. It is the juice, the food, the blossoming ingredients of all of our life's everything. These angels know that nature is their very selves an' are telling us that life breathes an' causes our movement. Angels are showing us the ways that make us function.

Thank you, sweet angel girl!

25

In My Light Home

I feel like twinkling away. I'm jumping up on little uni-corn's crystal, silver, diamond saddle, an' off we go galloping an' then flying faster an' faster till we set down in a land where shafts of Light are streaming up around little unicorn's shiny, glistening hooves prancing around so beautifully. Sparkles of my love are bringing us our arched, glistening entrance.

Little unicorn an' I are releasing fun colors around us. Lovely, sparkling, flying, winged little Light angels are appearing as we're continuing through this soft love drawing us deeper in as little unicorn begins vanishing right out from under me as I am now becom-ing these glistening fairy gardens, soft pink, yellow, an' blue circular domes where we fairies live, an' special entrances where us nature sprites come for fun to dwell. The beauty of our own company is so enchant-ing. This is my wondrous home. I'm thriving here with a peaceful, enjoyable relationship with myself.

Sweetness lives here along with happiness in a joining with my life's angelic food. My special place is made out of me. My diamond sparkling joining with life's angelic nectars that I've received an' used in my Light ways has become all this. As my Light takes me into my little actions, all things I do appear as my outer home. My home is solidly put together with purity attaching life in the same ways angels do. My thinking in starlight appears in tiny diamonds gathered together. These are sparks of my life's happiness.

I can think into a thing an' sun fly with any one of these small diamond sparkles. I then am reaching into my jeweled self. Life is like this. Complete freedom to be ourselves in our Light, a cocoon of forever peace in life's loving an' most kind ways of giving us lives filled only with life's heavenly correct ways. Yippy!

This is how angelic people have such a lovely, glowing look. It's made out of their inner love an' carefully released Light sharing. My life's jeweled home is my own livingness. Each of us brings our own self out of our thinking in Light. It's us. We are the beginning an' the ever continuing of our own world. A wonderful gift to ourselves we are, as our miracle ways continue.

I am sparkling away an' getting some rest today. It's so nice that little unicorn an' I ending up in my heavenly home. So fun sleeping an' drinking in angelic nourishment of my own life.

We always have this outer us, just as I have an outer level of my body that is on Earth writing all this down for my book on Earth. I join together with myself to share me with me. We are like sparkles within sparkles that form into circlets within circlets. It's just the ways we blossom.

We each have our own means of reaching through an' into our angel selves. Each one of us shows our self how. Our Light home is in us always. It is our very self, our diamond cloak we live in as we dart out of an' into places of Light within us. This place is a lovely me. I feel the softness of me being my best friend. A sweet feeling as life in me is living in a jeweled paradise. So nice. My unskilled an' damaged layers of me are also enveloped in my precious jeweled home.

My inner centers glow an' glisten. My skin is penetrated by the gold sparkles coming out of my gold reservoir mixed with diamond-silver sparks of eternity's goodies that I am made out of an' continue making myself out of. An' active swirl I am of the most precious life a person has ever seen. It's all me, you, we are swirling sunlight glistening our jeweled, kaleidoscopic, opalescent creation in our individualized angel selves.

It's so nice, you visiting my ways of being. Little unicorn is back, an' as we fly away my entire me forms into glistening pinpoints of diamond sparkles. Nature sprites, fairies, my sweet diamond home an' gardens are sparkling with me an' will be with me wherever I go. My life activates an' springs up into a way of living an' traveling in my star mind, glistens with some colors coming from beauteous, gentle friendships flowing from angel to angel.

Little unicorn stops at a river edge. We look out into living pastel swirls where we're seeing far into Light circlets that go deep within places of endless Light where miracle worlds are exciting fun Ever deeper we go into our own selves' continuous Light streams, always existing in peaceful tunes of forever's love.

Little unicorn is bringing me home now to where my earthly pen is becoming still. Jump into yourself. Your pools of love are awaiting your playful company.

26

Our Purity Source

Off we go giving streamers of love as our twinkle rainbow sparkles are dancing in sweet huggee lovees that are blossoming our purities into forever friendships. I love life so much. The more I love it, the better I feel.

Love is a reviving Light ointment. I put it on everything. It is fun pouring out love from me. There is only love that has sweet hugs in it. We are soaked in it. Feel it tickle you, huggee love you with its love breeze.

I found out what God is. God is huggee love! God is an active huggee love always on the move. Now that I know what God is, I feel better. God has been in huggee lovee land all my life. I just found out. Huggee loves go out through Heaven's Light swirling within us. It's God's buzzing around doing the God thing through a huggee love we share.

All my life I never saw God's moves. Who else could share such a feeling? Huggee lovees belong to God. Such purity in a huggee love. Purity is another word for God. Purity is in my huggee lovees. See, God stuff has that kind of purity, so I rename God in my heart "Purity." I can understand God better now because purity is busy huggee loving all of us.

27

Photos

People in my life, as I go along day to day, hear me talking about my family an' many a time say, "You should write a book about your family." That always sounds really nice.

Well, in my early life I never talk much, so know very little about conversations as I never got to have much chatting with people. So with no schooling, for me a book is looking for wings to just appear.

But somehow, some way, my life just begins to know things. I am just doing my life, an' it's all coming out of me just fine now. Life has a way about it to do what life feels it would like to do. How nice.

I love it this way. An' I do love life's ways. So I decided to put a little about my family in my angelic book. The photos do this for me.

Family an' acquaintances are the precious of my life. Also, my angel friends are the sweetest sparkles who bring into us an' our world angelic, sweet rising Light. So precious to be involved with angelic people. Remember, we are all becoming lots of Light as this rising Light gets more action into our beauty as we continuously sparkle-walk into our mind's heaven.

HUNT, WARNER DUANE, manufacturing confectioneer, b. Plymouth, N.Y., Dec. 3, 1868, s. Sylvester and Mary Jane (Harrington) Hunt. Ed. N.Y. State public schools and grad. Amherst College 1893. Mar. Florence Wuest, Oct. 6, 1901. Children, John Wuest and Warner Duane. Pres. Wuest-Bauman-Hunt Company; Prest. West. Res. Cond. Milk Co., V.P. Ohio Rubber Co., secy. and treas. Cleve. Chocolate and Cocoa Co. Mem. University and Cleve. Athletic clubs

he, his socialite mother and younger brother first joined the movement. The Hunts were at that time one of the richest and most influential families in the nation. Hunt's father, who died in the 1920's, was a millionaire industrialist.

ENTIRE FAMILY JOINED

The entire Hunt family joined Father Divine's cult convinced that the aging, balding little Negro with piercing eyes was God, Almighty. The Hunts turned over nearly every possession they owned to the movement, including property valued at tens of millions of dollars.

About the Pictures:
The top two pictures are my Grandfather an' his home on 70 acres. His son, my father, is the bottom picture.

WED IN SMOOTH CEREMONY

MR. AND MRS. JOHN WUEST HUNT were married Sunday afternoon at St. Matthew's AME Church in a beautiful ceremony which went off smoothly despite advance criticism from disgruntled sources. The bridegroom, who is nationally known as Prodigal Son, and his bride, were formerly affiliates of Father Divine.

Former Divinites Wed In Pretty Ceremony
Nuptials Lure 5,000

More than 5000 persons, half of them forming a solid, blockading mass of humanity outside St. Matthew's AME Church, 57th and Summer sts, were attracted to the beautiful wedding ceremony Sunday at 2 p.m. of Miss Florence Carole Street and John Wuest Hunt, both former followers of the Father Divine movement.

It was a double-ring ritual, dignified and restrained. Four prominent clergymen participated and the inter-racial bridal party included several well known individuals.

Thirty minutes before the bridal party arrived, all but 200 seats reserved for special guests had been filled in the 2200-seat capacity St. Matthew's Church. And every side aisle choked with standees. Outside, hundreds lined the sidewalks and streets awaiting a glimpse of the beautiful couple and their attendants.

A hush of admiration blanketed the assemblage as the bride alighted and the wedding party formed for their entrance. Escorted by W. Randy Dixon, newspaper men and radio commentator, who was to give her away, the bride presented an entrancing picture of loveliness and beauty.

She wore a heavy white satin gown, fitted at the waist, with full skirt. The sleeves were long with inserted valenciennes lace just above the wrist. The veil, bordered with valenciennes lace, was attached to a tiara of intricate design covered with seed pearls. Her train was three yards long. She carried a bouquet of gardenias.

Miss Ernestine Hughes was maid-of-honor. She wore a gown of blue mousseline-de-soie, sweethearted neckline, fitted waist and full skirt with inserts of valenciennes lace around the skirt and in the sleeves. Her headdress was a crown of blue flowers and veiling. She carried a bouquet of red roses.

Bridesmaids were Miss Barbara Thompson, Miss Eleanor Schrapf.

Continued on Page Twenty-three

About these Pictures:
My mom an' dad's wedding. Mommy an' Daddy met in this International Peace Mission. Mommy told Daddy what the

"I was one of Father

EDITOR'S NOTE: There have been millions of words written about George Baker, an obscure Baltimore handy-man who emerged on the national scene some years ago as Father Divine, a balding brown man who named himself God. Sometimes praised, more often denounced, we feel nothing written about him has ever approximated this shocking personal history of a white girl who lived in one of his "Heavens," was ravaged by the man she believed was a deity, and speaks forth now in the hopes that her words will provide a warning for others who might follow in her footsteps.

By CAROL SWEET HUNT

THERE ARE LOTS OF PICTURES of Father Divine, the Philadelphia "fire and brimstone" preacher who calls himself God. But none compare to the one etched in my memory.

It was a hot July night in 1942. Father Divine sent word for me to come to his office from my room upstairs in his Circle Mission church at 772 South Broad Street in Philadelphia.

Gruffly and matter-of-factly, as though he might ask for a cup of coffee, he told me to take off my clothes. For a moment that seemed like eternity, I couldn't believe my ears. This was the man who constantly admonished his thousands of followers to be modest and abstain from "pleasures of the flesh," lest they lose their souls.

I was a virgin, turned 21 by a few days. No other man in this world could have given me such a command. But to me he *was* God, or very close to it.

Obediently, I slipped out of my dress, took off my

He warns his followers that sex is the work of the Devil...but this blonde virgin learned that "Father" likes to break his own commandments

Continued about Mom an' Dad:

leader was doing to her an' the other girls. Daddy an' Mom left an' got married to tell on this leader. That's why there is 5,000 people at the wedding. These are a lot of ex-followers that also know what's going on behind closed doors. Before Mom met Dad, as Daddy says, he was railroaded into doing

Divine's Angels!"

shoes and began pulling off my stockings. Father Divine watched me with a smile on his face, then abruptly rose and walked into another room.

When he returned, Father Divine — this man I'd thought holy — was wearing only his shoes, socks and garters. His eyes glistened with lust.

This is my picture of Father Divine — the man who wrested from me not only a year's hard labor, not only practically every cent I had made, but also the most precious possession a young girl has.

Gullible? Stupid? Yes, call me that and more. But I wasn't the only one! Those sinful orgies with the "Angels" of his various "Heavens" went on all the time, daily in fact — and almost always with the white girls of his flock.

Had a Whole Harem of White Girls

Father Divine called me to his office on an average of once a month after that first night, to repeat the same shameful scene. Why not more often? I was shaken to the core when he nonchalantly explained it on one of those visits.

He had so many others—just like me—that this was as often as he could get around to me! What I had half-thought was something extraordinary with me had been but a common, everyday experience. The man had a whole harem of white girls. Much later, I talked to several of them; in each case, the routine had been the same.

By this time, you're wondering what on earth could have led me to participate, even unwillingly, in such things. The nightmare is easy to reconstruct.

I, Carol Sweet Hunt, a white girl of excellent family and good education, was brought to Father Divine's as a girl of 19 by my mother, who had somehow been hypnotized into becoming one of his followers. It was in May, 1941. *(Continued on page 64.)*

Young angels assigned to Father Divine's Circle Mission in Philadelphia found the place more like a harem than a "heaven."

35

Continued about Mom an' Dad:

a stint due to this leader's various shenanigans. Due to good behavior, Daddy says, 3 years rowing boats back an' forth from an' to McNeil Island is what he got for not playing the game of unfounded blackmail. Being railroaded, Daddy says, is an ugly twist.

"I WAS ONE OF FATHER DIVINE'S ANGELS"
Continued from page 35

Photo removed by the author, Kathy

York *Herald Tribune* reported that "members of Congress familiar with the situation said some of the homosexuals apparently had been 'protected' from questioning by former ranking officials of the Department of State."

If Sumner Welles, whose homosexuality was no secret in the White House, could rise to second in command of the State Department, it is not surprising that others who shared his weakness could rise to positions of rank, too. It is a chapter in American history that must not be repeated.

when Father still had a mission in New York, at 128th Street and Fifth Avenue, and mother decided to spend some time there. At her request, I went along.

I got my first taste of the man's awful power over other humans when it came time for mother and I to leave. Others at the mission came to us and told her that, unless she left me there—to become one of his novice groups, called "Rosebuds"—she and I both would die.

One of Divine's Favorite Tricks

That's one of Divine's favorite tricks — threatening destruction on those who oppose him. His devoted followers sincerely believe it, and mother was one of them. I was left behind.

Whether he had selected me, even then, as one of his future sex partners I shall never know. I settled down in the Fifth Avenue mission and, when law suits drove him out of New York State, I moved with him and dozens of his other "Angels" to the Circle Mission in Philadelphia on South Broad St.

There were no men there. Publicly, Father Divine denounces sex and the mingling of sexes. The mission was a converted hotel, where we girls slept two to a bed — always one white girl with a colored girl. Some of the larger rooms contained as many as four beds, occupied by eight girls.

Most of us worked hard for our room and board at outside jobs. For a year, I was a photographer's assistant at the Navy Yard and of the $1,600 I earned, I handed over $1,000 to Father Divine.

The "plum" jobs were as one of his secretaries, who worked only for Father. There was no pay involved — just room and board and whatever clothes he chose to bestow — but the jobs were eagerly sought and I felt flattered when I was eventually selected for one of them.

Later, I was to learn that was a sign Father had an eye on me. He watches his women followers closely to see that they obey his every order without question. Being made a secretary is the setup. Then he makes his move.

In my case, it started with frequent calls to his office, where he gave me long lectures about how he was God and, therefore, pure and clean. I not only listened, I believed. Occasionally, he would end these emotional sermons with a request that I kiss him. I always did.

It was a clever build-up, all leading to that ghastly night of July 25th, 1942. Today, it seems impossible to believe I ever submitted to his brutal, passionate first attack on me and even more incredible that I meekly returned to his office for repetitions.

Yet that was how I lived — for six years, cheated, despoiled and, I'm sure, laughed at by this wily scoundrel who masquerades as a man of God.

Girls Should Be Warned

It took me years to make up my mind to tell this true story of what happened to me and others I know who enlisted as his "Angels." Not that I was worried about those silly threats of supernatural retribution. But I'm a happily married woman with four children now; would such a confession darken their futures?

What decided me was the knowledge that other pretty young girls are walking into the same trap every day, fervently accepting this charlatan for what he claims to be. I think they should be warned that there's a heaven all right — but not under Father Divine's roof. I hope they listen.

Otherwise, for many of them, there'll come that night when Father Divine calls them into his office and ushers them onto the road — to Hell.

Continued about Mom an' Dad.

I'm glad I am sharing a little of my family's life. Sometimes, like my mom says, it's best to shine a little light to help others see the pebbles lying ahead. After all that this leader destroyed of Daddy's family's name an' riches, Daddy still is the sweetest, full-of-Light person I've known.

My dad, even now after he changed worlds, is a love contact to the beauty of my entire foundation of my life on Earth. I could always feel his comforting love. An' from the afterlife, our love is still just as much alive. The same goes for my mom. We chat, an' life continues.

But John W. Hunt insists that the standards by which other people live should not necessarily be the standards governing the lives of his family members. Indeed, that is the crux of his entire philosophy. His demand is to be left alone, to live the life of a perfectly "free" individual. And these desires are carried down into an intense battle against things such as public education.

About the Pictures:

This is my dad an' me. My brother, oldest sis, middle sis, an' me. I feel their love in me always. Then my daddy before I was in his life when he went to Harvard. Also, this is my mom. She is double jointed, an' I think she is so pretty. My mommy is the best an' kindest mommy.

About the Pictures:

My dad living it up at the hot springs. The hot water does spring up right there by the big rock. Daddy fishing. Me, Mommy, an' middle sis. Then Daddy always loving playing his ukulele. Then Mom canning. This is my most fun place.

.

28

Sweet Life

I am seeing a young unicorn. As I am little, around 6, a man is so nice an' is showing me where the horn comes out of little unicorn's head. I like this unicorn looking me in my eyes. Our feelings have so much to say as our eyes dance together.

This unicorn is not in the wild any more, but has a real nice old man as its keeper. I wish we all were living our natural life.

My Daddy goes to many jails. Daddy says about 30. An' 4 other places. He is tested to see what is up with him that he does break the law an' not send his kids to school. Daddy is keeping us kids out of the programming of the unnatural ways man makes life for all of us people. I keep feeling the love of a real life in the ways life is so fun to live in. Love an' joy I choose as my keeper.

It's fun, you being my forever sparkle friends. Sparkles of our lives are the breath of life for each other. You are the breath of life for me in many ways. This book of unicorns I have is so precious to me, seeing little unicorn's family ties. It's called *Unicorns I have Known* by Robert Vavra. I got it used online.

29
New Life

I can hold me like an angel,
I can love me like a charm.
I can keep me close an'
tender in my loving arms
to hold me like an angel,
to live with sweetness an' charm
as I dance this life together
in the sunshine of forever life.
I can hold me like an angel,
I can sing my songs of life
as I live in worlds of angels
dancing through the skies at night.
Loving every moment, I am together
in the pitch of forever life.
So I will keep loving me like an angel,
an' treating me like a charm,
bringing purity to me
in the sunshine of my inner life.
I can love me like an angel,
I can hold me like a charm.
I can love me,
I can hold me,
I can keep me in the Light.

Flying with My Golden Wings

For any sparkles you feel to share from your golden wings in love sharing, these are the ways: Kathy Darlene Hunt, P.O. Box 44, El Cajon, California, 92022, or use my PayPal email—kathy@kathydarlenehunt.com.

In my skilled Light, I know who you are. An' in your skilled Light, you know who I am. Life is our giver also. As we look to life, we thrive from miracle sustenance ways. Life cares about us. All of us. It's all okay. We are in the arms of life as it holds us firm. If you would ever like to drop me a line, it will be my fun.

Thank you for flying with me! See Ya.

A note from my life:

Everyone that is reading my book, I'm handing a tiny pink glowing rose releasing inner Light still attached to its heavenly roots. This rose's sparkling stem continues making its pinpoints of diamond Light so it does travel into any distance where it is taken. This rose always being attached an' alive, releasing its sustenance from this Lighted garden where it lives.

So as I ask you, return this rose back to my heavenly home as you're rearranging an' dissolving your earthly body, an' I will be aware of you in my heart's garden bringing me my pink rose. An' I will wrap my little angelic Light wings around you into your diamond memories that are coming alive as you're reaching into this black ink in my little book's life. An' I will be your friend in the Light of your angelic self.

. A child of the Light we surely are.

My middle sis will have a book. It's so fun for her bringing this book to life. Sis's name is Lynda Darus Hunt. She is calling her book *How I stay feeling young.*

James Goi Jr. is an author sparkle friend of mine, an' if you like, you can read his fun books that are sparkling with life's inner Light. Many ebooks are free online.

I feel so happy my first book blossomed. I would like life to pick up my pen again. Thank you, life.

P.S. We are dripping a sticky clear food feeding into us through an opening in our upper deeper area in our throat. Our kidneys are delivering our angelic life's liquids. Our colon distributes our air. Our inner attaching flow being the sun is what makes life happen.

The more inner eating an' drinking of our miracle solids, liquids, air, an' sun we rely on, the less physical eating an' drinking we will need to do.

Some of our miracle food leaks out in our water that we pass, is captured Heaven's food being used to heal skin, works for food an' water. Some droplets in water can clean hair, body, ears, an' teeth.

If these needs arise, nature can help even in the most barren of times where nothing is available other than one's self. We're wondrous an' understandable.